FOR JERROL,

I HOPE YOU FIN[...]
INFORMATIVE A[...]

WITH GRATITUDE,

Loretta Anne Woodard Verly

APRIL 2013

Being My Mom's Mom

*A journey through dementia
from a daughter's perspective*

By Loretta Anne Woodward Veney

Copyright © 2012 by Loretta Anne Woodward Veney

ISBN 978-0-7414-8210-5 Paperback
ISBN 978-0-7414-8211-2 eBook
Library of Congress Control Number: 2012923082

Printed in the United States of America

Published January 2013

INFINITY PUBLISHING
1094 New DeHaven Street, Suite 100
West Conshohocken, PA 19428-2713
Toll-free (877) BUY BOOK
Local Phone (610) 941-9999
Fax (610) 941-9959
Info@buybooksontheweb.com
www.buybooksontheweb.com

Table of Contents

Foreword

First, there were the conversations when, in the midst of speaking, she lost her train of thought. "Oh, it will come back to me," self-assured, she said, though I could hear the halting tone of uncertainty and frustration in her voice. Over time, she began to repeat herself, in many instances, word for word, over and over again. Unsettled, I said, "Mom, you just told me that." "Oh," she replied without any seeming conscious awareness of her repetition, then beginning again with what she already had shared. Within another too soon passage of time, came the shattering moment when I felt the need, *my need* to remind her, "Mom, this is Paul, *your son.*" "Oh, yes, hello, son," she responded, her voice, a tentative hush.

Then, my older brother died; my mother's grief ushering her more deeply into some distant sphere of existence separate from that state of consciousness of the pain of her loss. Then, within a year, my father died; he who, through his loving devotion to his wife of 53 years and in his care for his own sensitivities, kept from all, even those most near and dear, the secret of the depth of her deterioration. Then, came the confirming diagnosis: Dementia of the Alzheimer's type.

My wife, Pontheolla, and I were thrust, headlong and unprepared, into the world of elder care; a realm populated by an ever increasing millions upon millions of Americans. We also bore the disadvantage of distance.

We lived in Washington, DC, and my mother resided in her St. Louis home of 44 years, the one into which she, my father, and my brother moved the year I was born.

That was 1996. Since then, we have sought to navigate the deep and murky waters of elder care, involving the embrace of a multitude of responsibilities, among them, serving as medical and financial power of attorney (blessedly, my mother had authorized and signed those documents years earlier), contacting the Social Security Administration and the St. Louis Public School Retirement System (my mother was an elementary school teacher) to become her representative payee in charge of the receipt and use of her benefit payments, engaging in countless interviews, then the hiring of in house round-the-clock care givers, managing household expenses, and preparing annual personal and real estate tax filings. As year progressed to year, my mother's resources, adequate had she been able to continue to live independently, progressively fell short in the widening gap between her means and her needs.

In December 2010, after years of regular trips to St. Louis to look in first hand on my mother, repeated and deepening disappointments in the inconsistency in her care by some, but not all of her caregivers, the gradual disappearance of many of my mother's belongings, always "explained" with the caregivers' protests of personal deniability, and the expected, but still frighteningly increasing costs, we closed and sold my mother's home, moving her to a care facility in Maryland twenty minutes away from us. Now, we can see her more often, though it has been years since she, no longer conscious of herself or cognizant of her surroundings, could be present with us.

In the past two years, she has continued her physical decline. No longer "remembering" how to chew and to swallow, I have consented to the insertion of a "permanent" feeding tube, which has been replaced twice. Believing that this is not a life that my mother would have chosen for herself, although I would never want to promote her dying, still, I often wonder, indeed, second-guess myself about every medical decision I have made to prolong her existence. I also frequently, constantly ask myself, "What's next?" and "How long?" Neither question can I answer. What I do know is that each day we do the best we can with what we have to care for my mother, through whom I have life, as long as we can, which really means as long as she lives.

My story, though specific in detail to my circumstances of parentage and birth, aging and illness, is similar to anyone of the growing numbers of Americans charged with the care of their elderly loved ones. One such person is Loretta Anne Woodward Veney. She and her husband, Timothy, are two of my dearest friends.

Loretta is the author of *Being My Mom's Mom – A Journey Through Dementia From a Daughter's Perspective*, which, truly, is the proverbial labor of love. Through her recount of her life and of her experience in caring for her mother, Doris Woodward, Loretta, in a fluid and frank style, in parts, vulnerable and poignant, in others, witty and insightful, and, in still others, cautionary and advisory, offers to us the resources of help and of hope.

No one desires to be stricken with dementia. No one desires to be called to care for a loved one with dementia. Yet, with the advances in medical technology and delivery, one fruit of which is the prolongation of life, as we live longer, more and more of us are being faced with this dreaded reality. Loretta's chronicle is a guidebook, both generously loaded with practical information and graciously laden with uplifting inspiration.

Paul Roberts Abernathy
Washington, DC
November 2012

Introduction

My Mom, Doris Virginia Perritt Woodward was born on February 18, 1929 and diagnosed with dementia on March 17, 2006. I've thought about writing this book on my Mom's journey with dementia for the last few years, primarily because I miss my pre-dementia Mom. The Mom who was a great listener, who loved walking, Tai Chi class, and her friends and family, especially her parents Alberta and Charles, her siblings Donald, Frances and Diane, her son-in-law Tim, her granddaughter Nia, my sister Renee and me.

I hope this book will highlight the humor in this disease, humor that reveals itself along the journey at the most interesting moments, just when it is needed most. I also want this book to serve as a living document of my Mom's journey thus far, a journey which has been an incredible mix of her fierce independence, fear and anxiety and child-like innocence. While I'm hopeful that this book will be a source of help and comfort for others, I also realize that I'm writing it just as much for myself as for anyone else.

Before proceeding any further, let me share a few definitions concerning the basics of dementia.

Dementia is defined in Merriam-Webster's dictionary as a progressive condition marked by deteriorated cognitive functioning often with emotional apathy.[1]

The medical definition of dementia is a little more detailed, defined as a group of symptoms caused by the gradual death of brain cells. The loss of a few cognitive abilities that occurs with dementia leads to impairments in memory, reasoning, planning and behavior.

I'm an information junkie and love Google, so whenever I run across a word or term for which I need a definition or clarification, I Google it. Of course, learning about dementia is really scary, primarily because rarely is there a happy ending. Even so, I've learned as much about the disease as I possibly can because I am a true believer that knowledge is power.

The Alzheimer's Association website explains the four basic types of dementia as follows;

Alzheimer's disease (AD). The most common type of dementia, accounting for up to two-thirds of all cases, its cause is unknown and it is irreversible. Clumps and tangles of proteins develop among brain cells, interfering with their functioning and eventually destroying them. This usually begins in the memory and reasoning centers of the brain and eventually progresses to include the entire cerebral cortex (the "thinking" part of the brain).

Lewy body dementia (LBD). Round protein structures develop among brain cells for reasons unknown,

---

[1] Dementia. (n.d.) In Merriam-Webster Dictionary Online. http://www.merriam-webster.com/dictionary/dementia

displacing them and disrupting their functioning. LBD is increasingly considered the second leading cause of dementia, from twenty to thirty-five percent of all cases, but it is still considered a very new, relatively unknown classification.

Vascular dementia, is also known as multi-infarct dementia. Brain damage from narrowed or blocked arteries causes this condition, usually as a result of a stroke. The symptoms of this type of dementia depend on which parts of the brain were affected by the stroke. It had been the second leading cause of dementia, but has now been overtaken by LBD.

Frontotemporal dementia. In this form of dementia the brain's frontal lobes gradually degenerate, affecting a person's judgment and social behavior and appearing to alter a person's personality. It is a distant fourth in terms of overall dementia cases, yet is the second leading cause of dementia in people younger than age sixty-five[2].

Unfortunately, my research didn't provide a definitive answer about which type of dementia my Mom has. In some respects, given that the disease can be difficult to diagnose, I'm not surprised that I don't have an answer and I'm actually fine with not knowing. It's enough (sometimes too much) to know that she has the disease, so the specific details aren't really necessary.

According to the Alzheimer's Association, the financial cost of dementia can be considerable. Even though most

---

[2] Alzheimer's Association. 2012 Alzheimer's disease facts and figures. *Alzheimer's and Dementia: The Journal of the Alzheimer's Association.* March 2012; 8:131–168.

people with dementia are retired and not affected by loss of wages, the costs for family caregivers can be enormous due to lost wages, and the cost of medical supplies, drugs and safety modifications for the home.

One of the other reasons I'm writing this book is to help me with the emotional cost of dementia because the loss of many of the essential features of life and personality is one of the most difficult parts of this disease. It's the disease's unpredictability that requires the most flexibility and adjustments. Every single day can be different and requires that you learn to love each of the different people your loved one may become. I've already become more flexible than I ever thought I could be since I've become more responsible for my Mom's care.

There are many people I need to thank because it is impossible to deal with this disease without a very strong support system. First, I give thanks to my husband Tim for his unwavering care for my Mom and me. From the moment we were married, Tim has been more than willing to have my Mom come to live with us as he adores her.

Unfortunately, my Mom made a pledge to us on our wedding day that she would "not become a meddling mother-in-law". She not only has stuck to that promise, she took it to the extreme, rarely visiting us at our home. As my Mom's saving account began to dwindle due to the cost of her care, Tim volunteered to help regardless of the amount. Thankfully, my Mom still remembers Tim and always smiles broadly and says with confidence "HI, TIM!" whenever she sees him.

To my daughter Kim, who, although she hasn't had to help with my mother's care, has been a good sounding board when I'm feeling down. Kim's favorite question is "what can I do?" The answer so far has been "nothing", but I'm sure that will change in the future. I'm hopeful that this book can be a guide for Kim in the event that she has to become my "mom" one day.

To my Aunt Frances Beard (Frannie), who has been my rock through the years. Always listening to the things I couldn't tell my Mom, Frannie has been incredibly supportive of every single decision I've made regarding my Mom's care. We have such a small family, and I've relied heavily on Frannie's amazing historical knowledge of all sides of our family if I ever have questions or need information. I've learned so much from Frannie about my Mom that I would never have known without her. I'm beyond grateful that we've been so close for my entire life.

I thank my closest friends - especially Kris Lopez and Linda Vorgang, my two oldest friends and sisters from other mothers who are both the best listeners on my worst days and those I call or text just to laugh. They've both shared their kids with me too, blessing me with the gift and honor of being a Godmother. My Cha Cha sisters Mary Gilewski, Blanca Plaza, Emily Colon and Millie Luna, are the ladies in my life who are ready and willing to party at a moment's notice. During good and bad times, I can catch up with my Cha Cha sisters to have a glass of wine and be reminded of how lucky I am to have such great friends.

I thank the one and only Patricia Lusk, an incredible friend I affectionately called "Aunt Pat" who fought valiantly through several types of cancer in the ten years we were friends. We went through so much together and I learned many lessons from Pat about perseverance and positivity, even as she lived her last days in a hospice facility, leaving us on August 12, 2012.

I sincerely thank Vivian Adams, my Mom's oldest and dearest friend, who continues to reach out to and love my Mom in spite of her dementia. Mrs. Adams has been one of my biggest fans for my entire life, and I'm so grateful for her amazing love and support of my family.

The final two people I need to thank are an incredible couple. Paul Roberts Abernathy and Pontheolla Mack Abernathy are my family with a different last name. Paul not only is my brother, he's also an Episcopal priest and my Rector at St. Mark's Episcopal Church, Capitol Hill, in Washington, DC. We have had many conversations about dementia and Alzheimer's as both of our mothers suffer from the diseases. He truly understands my struggles and listens simultaneously as a pastor and as a loving friend. I've been truly blessed by Paul's guidance and support and his willingness to serve as my primary editor for this book. Paul's bride Pontheolla is my sister who is one of those incredible forces of nature. She is a truth-teller who puts everything in perspective. When it comes to my Mom, Pontheolla not only shares what she thinks, she also understands and cares how I feel. As an incredible gift to me, Pontheolla also has shared her wonderful mother, Geneva Watkins, with me.

Dealing with this disease is incredibly difficult and I can't imagine having to face it without my friends and family.

I dedicate this book to two strong women who left this earth much too soon, my Aunt Diane Perritt and my sister Renee Woodward Foote, and to my Mom Doris who is still on this earth with an incredibly strong body but an uncooperative mind. I pray that I've made them all proud.

Chapter 1 – Our Pre-Dementia Life

My Mom and I are complete opposites. From the day I was born, I've done everything at a fast and furious pace. I walk fast, talk fast, and work fast. I have lots of energy and am a very positive person. I have a wonderful husband and lots of friends. I am always "doing something". My Mom on the other hand, moved through her life at a much slower pace. She worked more than twenty years as a secretary in the Federal Government, and after retirement worked part time in retail and did volunteer work teaching children and adults to read. She certainly has friends, but was a fairly quiet person and never seemed very happy. My Mom had loads of anxiety too, about almost everything. She hated flying, riding in a car (because of the fear of other drivers) and being in crowds of people. However, although we were very different people, one of my joys as a child was the fact that I could always make my Mom laugh. Now that I'm an adult, we still laugh, but our roles are reversed. Over the last few years, having to make all the decisions regarding her safety and her care, I've slowly become my Mom's mom.

Our First Ten Years

I used to believe that January 3, 1959 would be a day that my Mom would never forget. It was the day that I was born in my grandparent's home in the Petworth section of Washington, DC. I was more than a month premature, so not only did I arrive unexpectedly in the middle of the night to be delivered by my father Lorenzo Anthony Woodward, but I also slept in a dresser drawer for a short period of time because my Mom had not yet purchased a bassinet. Today, my Mom remembers neither the date I was born nor my pretty exciting birth.

That said, there are many things that occurred when I was growing up that I'm thankful my Mom no longer remembers.

The main thing I'm happy my Mom has forgotten is my pretty interesting health history. Due to my premature birth, I was very sickly and in and out of doctor's offices and hospitals for quite a bit of my first ten years. I remember my Mom missing a lot of work because of me. The first time I was in the hospital was around age 4, due to some sort of urinary tract infection and a kidney problem.

I also remember that my Mom was able to make up the time she missed from work by going in early or staying late because I had a permanent babysitter in my grandmother.

I'm so grateful for the many sacrifices my Mom made for me AND for great medical insurance. Most of my mother's sacrifices were due to the fact that my father left home not long after delivering me and provided virtually no help in raising us, my sister Renee and especially me. Renee was nine years older than I and had the benefit of having our father in her life for that time. While my grandparents helped tremendously by babysitting us when necessary, my Mom took us to all our appointments and school meetings. I got the impression that my Mom went to great lengths not to take advantage of my grandparents in spite of the fact that she did pay my grandmother for her babysitting services.

When I was about the age of four, my Mom taught me one of the first and most important lessons: always help and serve others, always be kind, and never intentionally take advantage of others. The great thing about this lesson is that my Mom still remembers it and tells me often how kind, helpful and special I am. I've lived my entire life following this teaching, and the first time I remember doing something nice for someone else happened almost immediately.

If I was good, my Mom would treat me once a week to a High's ice cream cone. On one particular day, I received my ice cream cone at the same time another mother had bought one for her daughter. After we left the store, the four of us stood on the corner waiting to cross the street. For whatever reason, the other little girl's cone fell to the ground and she looked so sad. Without giving it a second thought, I handed the little girl my cone. Our mothers looked at each other in amazement. My Mom then bent down, gave me a big hug and told me I was special. Then she said, "Let's go get you another cone". Because it was a treat that I only received once a week, I told my Mom that I could wait until the next week because the other little girl needed the ice cream cone more than I did. I must have perceived somehow that the other little girl's mother may not have had the funds to replace her daughter's dropped cone. My Mom looked stunned. We went home and my Mom shared the story with my grandparents and my Aunt Diane and everyone commented on what an angel I was. I seemed to have been born with the ability to perceive what people need and when they need it, and try my best to deliver it.

I realized early on that my Mom seemed unhappy compared to other parents, but I didn't exactly understand why. I'm positive that most of my Mom's sadness as Renee and I grew up had everything to do with my father's departure. I also remember that when I was around the age of five I began asking where my father was. My Mom's answer at first was that he worked out of town, which satisfied me early on, but less so as time went on. The first time I understood that my father was not just out of town was when I became a Girl Scout Brownie. There were several father–daughter events and in spite of the fact that my grandfather always volunteered to take part with me, which I loved, I still wanted to know why my own father wasn't there. After asking her five or six times in a row, my Mom finally said to me in a very exasperated tone, "Your father isn't coming back, so stop asking me". I was stunned and hurt by her response, primarily because she didn't give me a reason. I was supposed to accept that he wasn't coming back because she said so. I didn't ask her anymore, but it certainly didn't stop my internal questioning.

Because I didn't have the real answer, I drew my own conclusions. My self-esteem dropped a little more each time I told myself that my father must have left because of me. In my mind, if he stayed around for nine years with Renee only to leave shortly after my birth, how could it not be my fault? Why else wouldn't my Mom tell me why he left us? I believed I had to be a very bad person if being born was enough to make my father leave forever. My Mom didn't hug us a lot, but if I didn't ask about my father, my Mom seemed much more affectionate. So I learned to accept what was and not to rock the boat. My life became one of pleasing others so they wouldn't leave me too.

The time of year I didn't have a self-esteem problem was, of course, Christmas, when like any other kid I was ecstatic. I was very spoiled in the sense that I received any and every toy and article of clothing I wanted, and then some, but I was also very appreciative of everything I received. One of my favorite toys was the Easy Bake Oven, which is really odd given that today I can't bake a thing. My Mom and I had a blast playing with the oven and she always encouraged me even if my baked goods looked and probably tasted awful. My Mom wasn't a good baker either, so I figured maybe it ran in the family.

The most bonding times with my Mom were the hours and hours she spent playing with me and my favorite toy, Lego building blocks. I received my first set of Legos for Christmas right before my seventh birthday. I was incredibly creative and built everything I could imagine. At several points in my childhood, I would have an entire table filled with my latest project. This was before many girls were playing with Legos, but my Mom always encouraged me to do whatever brought me the most joy and fulfillment. (Now that I'm an adult, because the amazing memories of building Legos with my Mom and grandfather are so powerful, I continue to use Legos today in my leadership and management training classes.)

Toys aside, the primary focus of the bond between my Mom and me was education. My Mom was a huge proponent of education and from a very young age she planted the seed that Renee and I would go to college. Actually, my Mom didn't just tell us we would be college bound, she said it was mandatory and advised us that we'd have to finish college before she would allow us to get married. I was fine with that, but Renee definitely challenged my Mom on that rule.

My love of education started when I was enrolled in nursery school at age two. Although I don't remember age two, the school directors told my Mom that I was really advanced for my age and that she should investigate the possibility of enrolling me in school early. My Mom did exactly that, and learned that early admittance to school required that I take a test. I took and passed that test, which happily allowed me to start school at age four.

Each year, all the way through my freshman year of college, my Mom took the day off from work on the first day of school. She'd be there in the morning with the camera as I left for school in my new outfit. She was there when I returned from school in the afternoon ready to listen to all my stories from my day. We started a ritual of going out to dinner on the night of the first day of school, primarily to a Hot Shoppes restaurant about 10 blocks from our house. During our walk to the restaurant and throughout our dinner, I talked and talked and talked about my teachers, the upcoming assignments, the books we were going to read, and all the supplies I was going to need. I also would set goals for every school year. After dinner we'd shop for any additional school supplies that the teachers requested at the Five and Dime store near our home. The first days of school with my Mom were priceless.

I didn't realize until I started writing this book how special those moments with my Mom were each year. I don't remember any of the outfits I wore or the names of my teachers over the years. What I do remember are the details from each of the years of the first day of school with my Mom. I could tell she was disappointed with herself that she never finished college, but still she was so intelligent and passed on so many great lessons to me, and gave me so much guidance and advice on selecting classes and term paper topics. She also was a wonderful listener as I shared at great length all of the information I wanted to include in my book reports.

Our Next Ten Years

One of the best experiences with my Mom in my pre-teen years was going to work with her when school was out. There was always something fun to do like photocopying and filing. If I worked really hard, I earned an awesome soul food lunch at a restaurant near her office. Lending my Mom a hand at work felt great to me because I knew I was really helping her, not simply doing busy work. Recently, I have realized that I got my work ethic from my Mom. She really liked the people she worked for and with and never seemed to have any bad experiences. The only thing I wish I could have changed about her work life was her compensation. She was a very low grade in the government and like many African-Americans of that time she never earned the level of pay she should have been given in light of the quantity and quality of her work.

There is something else that I've only begun to realize and appreciate in my adult years. That is the cultural experiences to which my Mom exposed us, even though she had very little extra money to spend. She always took us to the Smithsonian museums, free concerts, and the

Folklife Festival each year so we could learn about history as well as about other cultures. We also saved our change during the year so we could go on short family vacations in the summer. We went to places like Hershey Park, not only to ride the rides, but also to learn about how chocolate was made, and to Mount Vernon, George Washington's first home. I even had the opportunity to attend Girl Scout camp for three summers. As I think about it today, it probably was quite expensive for my Mom to afford, yet there I was having fun with all the other kids. The camps were memorable because I learned to do so many things I hadn't done before, including hiking, using a compass, building a campfire, and living off the environment.

My favorite summer trip was to New York City, an amazing place for my Mom to take Renee and me, given the degree of anxiety she had about so many things. To this day, I remember riding the ferry and visiting the Statue of Liberty and the United Nations. We also went to two Broadway shows and given the expense I am thrilled that Renee and I enjoyed them so much. I am amazed at how much my Mom was able to do for us even as a single parent.

My teenage years were a lot of fun, and my Mom was there for everything in which I participated. We had no car, so we went everywhere by bus or cab. There were Girl Scout outings and many high school activities – honor society, and newspaper and yearbook staff events. Whenever there was anything that required my Mom's presence, she was there even if the event was during work hours. It never occurred to me how difficult that was until I began working myself. I'm sure it was challenging getting time off during the day being the only secretary for several people in one office, but my Mom always managed to do it.

Birthdays were big events in our household and there was always a special family dinner and a grand cake. My thirteenth birthday was one of the best birthdays ever. My Mom and I always went out for dinner for my birthday, but on this occasion I got to invite a friend. As my guest, I asked one of the Clark sisters who lived next door to us for more than ten years. There were a total of eight children in that family and we were very close for the entire time we were neighbors and even after they moved to a different section of DC. I selected Leslie Clark as my dinner companion because she was already a teenager and I thought she could show me the ropes. I remember feeling really grown up that day. I also remember my gift from my Mom; a makeup mirror with lights, I was very excited about it, until we learned I was allergic to all makeup, including the non-allergenic kind. Still, I used the mirror every day as I combed my hair. I was so proud that my Mom gave me that mirror. I couldn't bring myself to part with it until I was in my forties.

Another great lesson I learned from my Mom was the value of saving money and buying only what I could pay for in cash. Growing up, I believed that everyone used department store layaway plans. Our favorite stores were Morton's and McBride's, where the clothing was good but didn't cost a fortune. By today's standards those stores would be the equivalent to Walmart or Target. When I found out that everyone didn't use layaway, I asked my Mom why we brought everything on layaway. Her answer has stayed with me for my entire life. She said, "When you use layaway, you own the items when you take them home because you have paid for them. When you buy items on credit, you may take them home right away and wear them, but because you haven't completed paying for them you are wearing something that you don't really own."

I remember my Mom having just a few dresses, blouses and skirts, and a few pairs of shoes that she wore to work over and over. She had a black pair of shoes, a brown pair and a pair of open-toe sandals for the summer. Renee and I on the other hand had plenty of clothes. Each season, my Mom would get us blouses or sweaters, and at least four of five skirts or pairs of pants. I had three pair of jeans as well. I had two pairs of shoes for school and one for church. My Mom made us feel as if we were rich because we never wore clothes that were falling apart and every item fit us perfectly. Everything my Mom bought for me, especially school clothes and Christmas gifts, was purchased using layaway plans and money from the Christmas savings plan at her bank.

Beginning in the summer after I turned thirteen, I applied for and received a work permit, and got my first job. In the afternoons and evenings in the summer and on weekends during the school year, I worked at the Smithsonian's Museum of History and Technology (now the Museum of American History) where I sold camera film and candy. I wasn't allowed to sell cigarettes or work in the cafeteria until I turned fifteen. I loved my job and having my own money. I opened my own savings account and bought my first ten speed bike with some of my earnings.

After I started my job, I talked my Mom into letting me join the Book of the Month Club, in which I maintained a membership for more than fifteen years. I loved to read more than anything else, and now that I could pay for my own library of books, my Mom allowed me to join the book club even though I was only thirteen. I was reading on the college level by then and when the Book of the Month Club magazine came each month, my Mom and I would read through the book reviews and recommendations and I'd make a decision about whether or not I would make a purchase. I looked forward to doing the book review with my Mom every month. One thing that really surprised me was that she put no restrictions on the types of books I could order. My Mom was very much old school and believed, for example, that girls shouldn't date until they were sixteen and that no revealing types of clothing should be worn in public. So I was sure my Mom would insist that I stick to reading the classics and that she'd never allow me to purchase any non-fiction books about sex or trashy novels. But I was wrong. Even though my Mom did a great job of explaining the facts of life to me and always told me I could talk to her about anything, there are always sexual questions that a teenager wants answered from someone other than her mother.

Some of the books I ordered and read were "Everything You Always Wanted To Know About Sex But Were Afraid To Ask" by Dr. David Reuben, "The Happy Hooker" by Xaviera Hollander, a simply amazing book that taught me I was not ready for sex as a teenager, and "The Stranger" by Albert Camus. I read all the time, especially on the bus ride to and from work. Reading helped to pass the time and opened the world outside of DC. I would never have survived all the reading in college had I not been motivated to read all the time as a teenager.

My high school years were life-changing. I attended Immaculate Conception Academy, an all-girls Catholic school in the Foggy Bottom section of Washington, DC. Had it not been for the sacrifice of my Mom and my grandparents, I never would have been able to attend. I was so thankful because the neighborhood public schools were too wild for me. To do my part to help offset the cost of tuition, during the summers I worked early mornings in the rectory of the Catholic Church attached to the school in order to earn free uniforms and books. In the afternoons, I went to my Smithsonian job. My Mom really had to trust me when it came to high school because it was about forty-five minutes from our house and required catching two Metro buses to get there. The only tricky part was transferring to the second bus. My Mom was a little worried because not only was I was almost two years younger than most high school kids, I also moved so fast that I'm sure she thought I'd get on the wrong bus at least once. Thankfully, the worry was all for naught as I never had any problems getting to or from school by myself.

Kathi Dawson, my best friend from high school, was always there for me for our entire four years and we simply did everything together from almost the first day we met. It was a very small school, so you really knew everyone and everyone knew you. My Mom loved Kathi, so she never was concerned about our hanging out together or worried about whether we would indulge in drugs or alcohol. That never happened.

What was an issue for my Mom was dating. She had a rule that my sister and I would not date until we were sixteen. Had my Mom stuck to that rule, however, I would have missed my high school prom. Thankfully, one of my other high school friends, Kim Cabness had a cousin named Joey Hawkins. My Mom liked him enough to allow him to take me out on group dates and to be my escort for the prom. My sister Renee had a fit that I was allowed to date before my sixteenth birthday, but my Mom explained that it wouldn't be fair for that rule to be the cause of me missing such a big event of my life especially given the fact that I worked so hard in school and was inducted into the National Honor Society. Joey and I dated all through high school. My Mom would ask every now and then if I was thinking of having sex with Joey. My reply was always that I wasn't interested in having sex with anyone yet, Joey included. My Mom seemed really relieved by my answer and she obviously believed me too.

One of the highlights of my high school years was being Renee's maid of honor in her wedding. I made all of the symbols that she wanted her bridesmaids to carry instead of flowers. Planning for her wedding was as close as Renee and I had been to that point in my life. Being nine years apart seemed more like a million years, as we never shared anything in common. I was happy to see Renee get married, but I wasn't sure my Mom and Renee would survive the years leading up to the nuptials. I always remember the two of them butting heads and arguing about almost everything, including boys, her grades, the fact that she lived with her boyfriend during college, and the year she would be allowed to marry. I, on the other hand, never argued with my Mom and I was definitely her favorite child though I was never sure why. On reflection, maybe I should have argued with my Mom, at least enough to find out more about my father; an important person about whom I believed I had a right to know.

One of the most important times in any teenager's life is learning how to drive. My best friend Kathi was the person who took on that task for me and she was a great teacher. Her parents had given her a Chevy Camaro for her sixteenth birthday and she was nice enough to share her gift with me by letting me drive sometimes and picking me up for school many days. When I turned sixteen, I was very excited to get my driver's license, but I don't know what the rush was because there was no car at home as neither my grandparents nor my mother ever learned how to drive. In my Mom's case, that was probably a good idea given the level of anxiety brought on by simply riding in a car.

My sixteenth year was also the time that a wedge was driven between my Mom and me because of two incidents that changed our close relationship for a considerable period of time. Though we never talked about my father, I always wondered why he didn't pay child support like other dads. I also wanted to know where he lived and why I had not met him. One day, one of my Mom's friends told her that my father was working at Howard University, a mere ten minutes from our house. Immediately, I asked when I could see him and my Mom said I couldn't. When I asked why, she said because we don't always get what we want and that I should be happy with the life I had. That didn't make me happy at all, but I tried to keep my hurt inside.

As none of the adults in my life were giving me the answers I was seeking, I did the next best thing and tried to find my father on my own without my Mom's knowledge. This was the first incident that caused a problem between the two of us. My friend Kathi and I went to Howard University every day after school for about a week, and sat outside the building where we believed my father worked, waiting and watching for someone who looked like me. I had been told for most of my life that I looked exactly like my father. Unfortunately I never saw him and it took me forever to get over that disappointment. I often think today about what I would have done if I had seen him. What would our time together have been like? What would we have said to each other? When my Mom found out that I had gone looking for my dad on my own, she was furious and reprimanded me. It was the worst punishment ever. I was planning to have a big sweet sixteen party complete with boys. Instead I only could have a few girlfriends over from school. I was crushed but at least happy that I was allowed to have friends over for lunch and, of course, a birthday cake. My Mom seemed most upset that I had gone behind her back. She told me that she no longer trusted me and accused me of being ungrateful for all she had done for me. There was so much I didn't understand, especially how simply wanting to get to know and spend time with my father made me ungrateful. I was definitely grateful for everything my Mom had done for me, yet I felt like half of me was missing. If my father had been dead, that would have been different and I would have accepted that. But that was not the case. My father was alive and well, yet we had no relationship. Years later, I would come to understand why my Mom was so angry with me.

The second incident that created a barrier between my Mom and me occurred when I became great friends with a twenty-one year old gay woman from Brooklyn, New York. She came to DC every summer to stay with her cousins who were our neighbors. We spent a lot of time together during the summer talking and listening to music, and during the school year, we wrote letters to each other. After I received the sixth or seventh letter in the mail from her, my Mom insisted that I end the relationship. When I asked why, for my Mom was open to all of my friends, her only reason was that my friend was too old for me. I thought that was ridiculous because all my friends were older than I was. I did not understand my Mom at all. She seemed so angry about a very innocent friendship. It was as if she thought I was gay too. I remember my Mom not speaking to me for days at a time over this issue. I finally gave in and stopped writing my friend, which saddened me because we had absolutely no romantic interest in each other. Although I didn't have a lot of experience with boys, I knew I wasn't gay.

Junior year of high school was very interesting. As a bright student with a history of accomplishment, I believed I could get into any school I desired, so I toured all of the colleges in the Washington, DC area. In the end, having gone to Immaculate Conception Academy for high school, Catholic University seemed the most logical choice for me. Not only was it a great school, but was just the right "size" for me. I was also admitted to a university outside of the DC area, but decided against going there because I was afraid my Mom would be too sad if I left home. She seemed more sad than usual as I neared the end of my high school years. So I thought if I stayed in DC for college, I could fix everything and my Mom would be happy again, at least as happy as she could be. Delighted, I accepted admission to Catholic University.

The greatest sacrifice my Mom made for me during high school was to allow me to go with the French Club to

Quebec, Canada. It was the first time I had been that far away from home. Because of my excellent grades, I was the only junior allowed to go on the trip. I actually used some of the French I learned in class to order food from a menu and to understand much of what our tour guides shared with us. I called home several times recounting for my Mom all the details, all the "sights and sounds". I was homesick, but I enjoyed every minute of that wonderful opportunity.

My senior year was somewhat boring as I had finished all my course work in the first quarter. I was given advanced work to keep me busy for the rest of the year so I'd be even more prepared for college. Graduation was thrilling and the entire family celebrated with me. I couldn't wait for college to start!

I thoroughly enjoyed my time at Catholic University. I credit my Mom with preparing me to interact with people of all races and cultures. When we attended the freshmen weekend orientation, Mom and I were the only African-Americans in attendance, but we didn't dwell on it, and I never felt uncomfortable because I had been around people who didn't look like me for my entire life. I made many friends and my Mom encouraged me to take advantage of every opportunity presented to me. As I was a decent writer, my Mom encouraged me to join the newspaper staff. I was accepted immediately and welcomed with open arms. In my capacity, over my four years, I was fortunate enough to get some of the biggest stories on campus, including the 1980 visit of Pope John Paul II just weeks before my graduation. My Mom kept every article I wrote and she and my grandparents showed the Catholic University newspaper to all the

neighbors as if I was on the staff of a Pulitzer prize-
winning publication.

Our Life From My Twenties Through My Forties

My Mom and I shared good and bad times in my first
twenty years as an adult.

Because I had started school early, I received my Master's
Degree from The George Washington University in DC
before by my twenty-first birthday. My graduations were
fabulous celebrations for our family. One weekend was
especially exciting as Renee received her Master's Degree
from Trinity University and I received my Bachelor's
Degree from The Catholic University. The two
universities are less than a mile apart and as the
graduations were at different times of day, the entire
family could attend both ceremonies. It was one of the
most memorable weekends I ever shared with my sister.

After I obtained my private investigator's license when I
turned twenty-one, my Mom learned through an
educational event at work that my father was living in
Jacksonville, Florida. I was able to locate his address,
which allowed my Mom to finalize the divorce. I was
hopeful that I'd get to see my father when he came to DC
for the legal proceedings, but that didn't happen. As my
parents had been separated for such a long period of
time, he simply had to sign the relevant documents. I still
didn't understand what happened between my parents. I
had learned so much in college and grad school, but still
hadn't learned the answer to the biggest question in my
life: Why didn't I have a relationship my father?

The greatest thing that happened in my twenties was meeting Tim, a Washington DC police officer. Tim and I met during a bomb threat of all things. While completing my Master's Degree in Criminal Justice/Forensic Science at GWU, I had a work study job in the Student Center. I answered the phone and was stunned that the person on the other end of the line was threatening to blow up the building, one that housed several thousand people. The University believed that the situation was serious enough to call the Metropolitan Police and Tim was one of the officers who responded. When he asked for my phone number, I assumed he needed it for the case, and while that was true, he was also very interested in dating me.

Prior to meeting Tim, I hadn't dated for more than six months after my fiancé Tommy left me alone in a hotel room on the day we were supposed to be married. Because he had taken all of my money, I had to call Renee to rescue me. Renee and my Mom were very supportive of me. It was the only time I ever had reached out to my sister. Usually I was the one responding when she needed help. As I never shed a tear at Tommy's departure, I felt he wasn't the man I was to marry. Truly, I was more upset that he took my belongings. Later, he professed to me that he believed he wasn't good enough for me and decided to leave me so that I might have a great life. I wish he had just told me that. My Mom probably had doubts about whether Tommy was the person for me, but she never shared them. While she felt really sorry about how the relationship ended, she also was relieved that I wasn't marrying him. When Tommy left, I thought I was done with men, however after the first couple of dates with Tim, I knew he was the one for me and the rest, as they say, is history. When I first told my Mom that Tim was thirty years old, she was very concerned about the nine year difference in our ages. But once she met Tim, she simply loved him and instantly gave her approval of our relationship.

When Tim and I had been dating for about a month, my Mom and I had a conversation about him that was life-changing for me. Because I didn't have a car, Tim would come by in the mornings after his midnight shift on the police department and drive me to work at GWU. One morning I was waiting for Tim and he was about fifteen minutes late. I was terrified that something terrible had happened to him. I was pacing the floor and crying. My Mom asked me to sit down for a minute and told me to think about how I felt at that very moment. She pointed out that if I continued to date Tim, I'd be living the kind of life where I'd always be waiting for him to come home from a dangerous job. She told me that I either needed to suck it up and stop crying, especially given that I hadn't received any bad news or I needed to stop seeing him. As I had no intention of ending our relationship, I remember nodding, getting up, drying my tears and then waiting calmly for Tim to show up. Turns out, he was hanging out for a few minutes after work with the guys. After that talk with my Mom, I never again became hysterical if Tim happened to run late. That conversation with my Mom was some of the best advice she ever gave me. It kept me grounded and well prepared for the thirteen remaining years of Tim's twenty-three year career in law enforcement. During his time on the force, we faced several police car accidents, a dog bite, and his being shot at, but remembering that talk with my Mom I remained calm through it all.

When Tim and I got married in 1985, my grandfather gave me away, just as he had given Renee away at her wedding. I was thrilled, BUT had dreamed many times of my father showing up at the last minute to walk me down the aisle. I knew it was wishful thinking, but in response to a letter I had written to him six months before my wedding day, I had hoped he would. In that letter I told him all the things I had done in the first twenty-five years of my life, including my engagement to Tim and about our daughter Kim from Tim's first marriage. I was really disappointed that he made no reply, but my life moved on. The only people on earth who knew I had written to him were my aunts Frannie and Diane. My Mom probably would have had a fit had she known.

My late twenties and all of my thirties were by far the most difficult period of my life as I battled an extremely serious case of endometriosis, which typically is not a serious disease for most women. The primary symptom of my endometriosis was intense, almost unimaginable pain, at times, forcing me, in an attempt to seek even marginal comfort, to crawl on my hands and knees.

Once the cause of my physical anguish had been diagnosed as extensive endometriosis, the surgeries began to remove it and repair my badly damaged internal organs. My entire team of doctors led by my gynecologist, and including a general surgeon, a urologist, a nephrologist and a gastroenterologist, worked tirelessly for thirteen years to cure me. Even though I was the one who was sick, my Mom took this period in my life very hard. She blamed herself for the fact that I was born prematurely, and for not taking me to a different doctor when I began to have horrible cramps around my nineteenth birthday. Of course, none of this was my

Mom's fault. As we were not doctors, we accepted what we were told, that nothing unusual was wrong with me. When I became an adult, I selected my own gynecologist, who also convinced me that there was nothing seriously wrong with me. Even then my Mom continued to hold herself accountable.

I didn't know how hard this time was on my Mom until very recently when Vivian Adams, one of her best friends, told me how much my Mom cried and suffered during each of my nineteen surgeries. During that time period my Mom took a lot of time off from work, both from her government job before she retired, and from her part-time retail job after retirement in order to be at the hospital during the operations, and with me at home after my discharge from the hospital. I was determined to live through this illness because I didn't want my Mom to have to bury me. She had already grieved over my father's departure, what would she do if I "left her" too? One of the most difficult things I ever had to do was to tell my Mom that I needed another operation. There were several years that I had three or four procedures annually. Each time I learned that another surgery was needed, I would practice explaining it to my Mom without having any fear in my voice. I tried always to be upbeat and positive so my Mom would not know how afraid I was. Once I was standing in front of my Mom and explaining what the next surgery would involve, her eyes would get bigger and she would sigh more deeply. I'd say "We've been here before, we'll get through this" and she'd say "You've been through so much already I wish I had your positive attitude". I wasn't always that positive, but tried to be so for my Mom and Tim.

During all of my years of illness, my Mom and Tim worked closely together whenever I came home from the hospital. Tim would cook and take care of the house, and my Mom would change my bandages, help me shower and dress every day, and lend a hand with my physical therapy. The two of them became very close, sharing their hopes and their fears, especially when no one, including the doctors, was sure I was going to survive. My Mom, in her efforts to be of help to me and to us, stayed with us during those times. Throughout our marriage, she never came just to "visit", there had to be a purpose.

One of the most pivotal events in my relationship with my mother occurred in 1990. She summoned Renee and me to a meeting and, because she never had done this, I knew right away that she was going to tell us that our father had died. That was precisely the news my Mom delivered to us. Immediately Renee began to cry while I sat stoically. For some reason I couldn't cry for someone with whom I never had had a conversation, someone who clearly had not wanted to meet or be in relationship with me. But my father's death was only the beginning of the story. My Mom then dropped the bombshell that the reason he had left us all those years ago was because he was gay. So this was the big secret, the reason he never met me? That was crazy! Many people's parents were gay and yet they still were a part of their children's lives. Why didn't my Mom share this information when she was teaching me the facts of life? Seems to me that it would have fit in well.

After hearing that second piece of news Renee cried even harder. I still just sat there feeling as if I had been shot in the heart. My dream of sitting down and having a conversation with my father had ended. I felt so cheated, because the man who had delivered me, whose personality, looks, mannerisms, intelligence, and sense of humor I had inherited had been kept from me for no reason other than the fact that he was gay. My Mom had learned of my father's death from someone from the old neighborhood, but she arrived at DC General Hospital after they already had cremated his unclaimed body. Thus even after his death, I still didn't get to see him. I was so hurt but I managed to listen calmly to the rest of my Mom's "speech", which she clearly had rehearsed, and left after saying very little to either my Mom or Renee. I tried not to be too angry with my Mom, because she obviously had never gotten over my father leaving her for another man. Still, truly, I was angry with her. So many questions about my life were answered during that meeting – namely my Mom's perpetual sadness, her insistence that I end my friendship with my gay friend in NY, and especially her demand that I never try to find my father. The only freedom I felt on that day was that so much more of my life made sense.

After the family meeting, my Aunt Diane called wanting to know what had been discussed. At first I said I couldn't tell her because my Mom asked us not to divulge any information to anyone, but as my aunts and I had no secrets, I told her. Diane's response? "That's not news, everyone knew he was gay!" What? Everyone knew? Apparently when my parents married, everyone except my poor Mom knew that my father was gay. At that moment, I felt a little more sorry for my Mom. It took me weeks to process all the news my Mom had shared, and even writing it down now brings back a variety of emotions for me.

Not long after the news of my father's death, both my grandfather Charles and my father-in-law Lawson, two men I adored died. Their deaths took an incredible toll on me, especially since I was the one who had to tell Tim about his dad's death. My brother-in-law Michael died the week before my father-in-law so it was a very sad time. After my grandfather's death, my focus turned to my grandmother and my Mom. I was worried how the two of them would fare in that large row house without a male presence. In spite of the fact that my grandfather was in his eighties when he died, he still did a great deal around the house. I wasn't worried about their safety because I knew the guys in the neighborhood, who my grandmother and mother had known for their entire lives, would look out for them.

I began to pay a great deal of attention to the relationship between my grandmother and my mother who began to take over her mother's care, accompanying her to doctor's appointments and ensuring that she took her medicine as prescribed. My Mom took great care of my grandmother, yet I felt that since they had lived together for all of my Mom's adult life, she also seemed to have some anger and resentment because of the weight of her new responsibilities as a caregiver. I began to notice that if my grandmother said something more than once or didn't take her medicine in a timely fashion, my Mom, at times, would yell at her. It caused me to wonder how I would be if I had to take care of my Mom. Renee and I had that discussion on more than one occasion. I had vowed that I would never lose my patience with my Mom. Inherently, or so it seemed to Renee, I was the patient one between the two of us. Moreover, as my relationship with my Mom had been much better than had been true for Renee, we decided that while we both would help with my Mom's care, I would be the primary caregiver for my Mom if that became necessary.

Then in 1998, my Mom took my grandmother to the doctor because she had been complaining of stomach pain. At first, my Mom didn't seem to believe that anything serious was wrong, but after she continued to complain, a trip to the doctor revealed colon cancer. My grandmother had surgery and we all rallied around her. The four of my grandmother's children and the nine of us grandchildren all helped out as much as we could with her care. When my grandmother decided that she wasn't going to do any chemotherapy or radiation, we began to focus on what would make her most comfortable. She decided that she wanted to die at home. So I followed the ambulance from her temporary nursing home back to the home in which I was born many years before. My Mom and Aunt Diane became my grandmother's primary caregivers. Diane, Renee and I attended a class at the hospital to learn how to change my grandmother's colostomy bag. I felt really useful and was happy to help my grandmother after all the years she had cared for me as I was growing up.

My Mom was very quiet during this time. Although lots of people came over to see my grandmother as her cancer progressed, my Mom didn't engage or share much about what she was feeling, at least not with me. As I think about it now, I didn't share my feelings with my Mom. When it became obvious that my grandmother's time on earth was getting short, we called in the hospice care folk, who were most professional and compassionate. One of the most moving moments came when the family gospel group of my ex-brother-in-law, Renee's former husband

Bruce, came to sing for my grandmother. Bruce wanted to do something special for my grandmother because my grandparents allowed Renee and him to live in their house for more than a year while they saved money for a house. As the group sang popular spirituals, my grandmother was said to be in a coma. We were all standing around her bed enjoying the music, when all of a sudden my grandmother began singing along to the words of her favorite hymn without opening her eyes. Everyone in the entire room was crying. I had not experienced anything like that in my life and have known no such moment since. I was thrilled that though Bruce and Renee had a very difficult divorce, he and his siblings still came to sing for my grandmother. That gesture on their part was appreciated by our family beyond the power of our words to express. My grandmother died the next day with my Mom and my Aunt Diane by her side. I got there a few minutes after she expired, but before the funeral home came to pick up her body. I wept uncontrollably when I saw my grandmother lying in the bed. My Mom didn't seem to know what to do, so my Aunt Diane came over to comfort me. My Mom looked as if she was in shock, but said very little.

Renee and I were very worried about my Mom living in the big house all alone, but all the neighbors kept an eye out for her. A year after my grandmother's death, my Mom and her three siblings agreed to sell the house, that sacred place of my birth, "as is" and split the money four ways. While the house was on the market, Renee and I helped our Mom search for a retirement apartment. After visiting more than ten residences, we finally decided on a place called Friendship Terrace in the Friendship Heights section of DC. It had a good number of activities, but wasn't too big, or with too many people. In September 1999, my Mom moved to the fifth floor of the building. Renee, my niece Nia, and Tim all helped to move my Mom out of the house she'd lived in for almost 40 years, and into this strange new place. The building had everything, including a great activity room, a library, a beauty salon, laundry room, and a nice cozy dining room where everyone knew your name. It was walking distance to almost anything you could want – a pharmacy, a bank, two grocery stores, a small shopping center, a huge senior center, a public library, and several great restaurants. Renee and I felt as if we had picked the perfect place. I wondered if this was how parents felt when they were picking schools for their kids. I knew how important this decision was. My Mom was perfectly fine with all of us deciding together where she would move, as long as the place was in Washington, DC, the city of her birth and the only place she would consent to live. Her parents, native Washingtonians died there and my Mom planned to do the same. No pressure on us! I was thrilled that not only was her studio apartment great, but it was an Episcopal retirement community too. Both my Mom and I are lifelong Episcopalians, while Renee had converted to the African Methodist Episcopal (AME) church when she became an adult.

As we moved my Mom's last few things out of the house, I was incredibly sad. Renee couldn't bring herself to come on the last day, so Tim and I finished the move. I understood how Renee felt, as it was the only home I had known until I was married. I thought that house, which contained so many memories, both good and bad, would always be in our family. Now someone else would be living there. I had taken lots of pictures, but I also wanted a piece of the house too, but that wasn't to be. My Mom didn't seem sad to be moving, and I wondered why. Could it be because she had NEVER lived alone as an adult until now?

I was delighted for my Mom because she seemed really happy. She jumped into all of the activities at her new place. There were church services, educational classes, book club, field trips, rummage sales, and sandwich-making for the homeless which she did each week. To keep her body in the same shape as her mind, she took stretch and flex exercise classes and began Tai Chi.

My Mom had never been this socially active in her entire life, and I was surprised to see her doing so many things. It was almost like she had been freed from some prison. Had her life with her parents for all of her adult years been that bad? I wasn't sure, but it was great to see my Mom so vibrantly engaged. We thought she'd be miserable at first, but she was anything but that. My very quiet Mom even signed up to take prospective new tenants on a tour of the building. Who was this woman? I was blown away by the fact that my Mom seemed so alive!

Renee and I were called Sponsors in my Mom's new community, and they encouraged us to participate in as many activities with her as we could. I was able to join in many of the pursuits, for, at the time I worked less than five minutes from her building. Renee couldn't take part in as much because of her very full life of work and active engagement in the ministries of her church.

Even through my serious illness I hadn't seen Renee much at all, unless my Mom called her encouraging her to visit when I wasn't doing so well. Whenever my Mom requested her presence, Renee would come. After years of communicating mostly on holidays, I finally reached out to Renee and suggested that we have monthly sister days. For her 50th birthday in 2000, I took her on a cruise to the Caribbean. We had a great time, although we still didn't come away with the tight sister bond as I had hoped, it was at least a start. My Mom was thrilled that Renee and I took that trip, as she wanted us to have a great relationship as adults. I never knew that that trip would be the only one my sister and I would take together.

For the first five years of my Mom's residency at the retirement community, all went very well for the three of us. Renee, our Mom, and I shared outings, trips, and holidays. Then in early 2004, something began happening with Renee. She was complaining of dizziness, and blurred vision, especially at night. I became so concerned about Renee's poor vision that I had to insist that my Mom no longer ride with her. I took her to several doctors, and at first they believed that she had suffered from macular degeneration. When an eye specialist determined that was not the case, many other tests were conducted.

Renee began to exhibit other symptoms too, like numbness and weakness. The doctors still weren't sure exactly what was wrong, but they kept hinting that it might be multiple sclerosis. By late 2004, Renee finally decided to take her daughter up on her offer to move to California where they could spend more "quality time" together. I packed up Renee's entire house, which was headed toward foreclosure after she, having lost her vision, was fired from her job. After taking care of all the bills we sold her house and got her ready for the cross country flight.

When I accompanied Renee to California in March of 2005, she only had a cane and was still searching for a diagnosis for all of her symptoms. On the morning before we headed to the airport, Renee thanked me for everything I had done for her, and then made a startling confession, telling me that she had been a terrible sister to me for all my life. I was grateful for her admission, but sorry that it took a serious illness and her moving away for us to address some of the issues in our relationship, which had so much to do with my father's departure. Years earlier, Renee had confessed that she had blamed me for our father's leaving and for being our Mom's favorite child. My Mom was very worried about Renee, because none of the possible diagnoses we were hearing about were good. Finally in late 2005 came the official verdict, Renee had MS. When I told my Mom, she was silent. If she cried, she didn't do it in front of me. I was worried, because without Renee here in DC to help me, I now felt like a single parent who'd be taking care of my Mom alone. It was a scary thought. I also wondered how Renee would fare with this disease. My worry was warranted, as her disease progressed very quickly. Renee moved from her cane to a walker to a manual wheelchair to an electric wheelchair to a hospital bed that I brought for my niece's apartment to a nursing home in less than four years. I tried to keep Renee in the loop, including her in all decisions regarding our mother's care. I wasn't sure how to assist Renee other than a little financial assistance in the form of grocery gift cards. I decided a great way to help would be to sign up for the MS Marathons, which are two day 50K events that raise money to find a cure. I did my first marathon in September 2006, and when I visited Renee a few weeks later I gave her the medal I received for walking, which seemed to really inspire her.

In spite of my realization that Renee would be unable to help me with my Mom when she got older, I still believed that I'd have my Aunt Diane, my Mom's youngest sister seventeen years younger, to help me. I knew Diane would be here forever because she was such a lover of life! But that changed too when she was diagnosed with stage four colon cancer in February of 2006. She chose not to take any treatment for it and was given six months to live. I was stunned! When she called me and asked me to come see her, I knew it would be bad, but I didn't imagine it would be as terrible as it was.

When Diane told me she was dying, she also insisted that I not cry, so I didn't. She planned her entire funeral service while I sat there, informing me that I would give the eulogy, just as I had for my grandmother in 1998. I simply said "OK". I then drove my aunt to tell her siblings that she was dying. It was one of the hardest jobs I've ever had to do. When we got to my Mom's apartment, she was stoic. I remember her saying, "Oh no," but not too much else as my aunt did most of the talking. My Mom seemed deflated, just as we all were, but she kept her feelings to herself, as she did most of the time. After getting hospice involved, my cousin JoAnne, and my aunt's dedicated co-worker/ adopted daughter Michelle, and I took care of my aunt until the end.

When Diane died in August of 2006, it was one of the worst days of my life. She was everything to us. She was the cool aunt, who because she was fairly close to my age, only thirteen years older, took part in all the fun activities, for example going to amusement parks and riding all the rides. She allowed us, all my cousins and me, to have parties with very loud music. She kept us together by taking us on weekend trips and giving the best advice. She supported us in every possible way and attended every special event in our lives. I remember getting elected to the Student Council in the 5th grade. It was no big deal at all, but there was my Aunt Diane and my Mom sitting in the audience at the recognition assembly.

My aunt was so young at sixty years of age, how could she be dead? Not only did I lose my aunt that year, but her death also marked the beginning of a change in my Mom too. I noticed it right away at Diane's wake prior to the funeral. As we viewed the body as a family for the first time, we were all fairly composed. My aunt looked simply beautiful in the suit I had picked out for her the day before. As we stood around the casket, I heard a loud wail. I wondered who it was. I looked around and my Mom was no longer standing next to me, but trying to rush out of the viewing room. She had not made it before she started to cry. I had never seen my Mom cry like that in my entire life. I just hugged her, but I don't remember sharing any words with her in that moment. My Mom kept repeating over and over, "I'm the oldest and I was supposed to die first. She was the youngest." I felt horrible that I couldn't say anything to make it better. My Mom was never the same after that. She had already been diagnosed with dementia by the time Diane died, but the symptoms got worse after my aunt's death.

It was the little things at first.

Chapter II – It Was The Little Things At First

I'd share something very important with my Mom and before our conversation ended, she would ask me a question about what we already had discussed. I was hurt that she didn't remember what I had said, for I thought she was simply tired of listening to me talk. (I can out talk most people even on my bad days.) It never occurred to me in the beginning that all was not well with my Mom.

After Renee had the same experience with our mother, we talked briefly about what it might mean. We decided that as our Mom was getting older, maybe we needed to have important conversations with her in person as opposed to over the phone. Maybe she was trying to multi-task while on the phone with us causing her to forget what we talked about even when it was important. I smile when I think of that discussion today, for it simply did not occur to us that something could be seriously wrong.

It was the little things at first.

We would go to the grocery store and my Mom would not remember the date that she needed to write on her check. Several times, even though we always went to the same store, she couldn't remember on which aisle a particular item was located. That may not seem like a big deal, but my Mom is a creature of habit. She bought the same brand of the same items every week, even if a different brand was on sale. Not being able to remember where to find always purchased items should have been a key for me. At first, thinking how odd it was that she forgot the layout of her favorite store, I would remind her, saying, "You're really distracted today."

She would leave blank a section of a check that needed to be filled in and mail the bill anyway. When the check would be returned to her as incomplete, my Mom would explain it by saying she was busy at the time she wrote the check and her mistake was simply an oversight. She then would fill in the blank area; or write a new check. To my knowledge, she never was penalized for a late payment.

I tried to have dinner with my Mom as often as I could, especially when Tim was working late. One of the things my Mom loved most about her building was the dining room dress code: no t-shirts, shorts, jeans, or flip-flops allowed. Everyone looked lovely arriving for dinner. As my Mom required no assistance, her dinner time was the later seating (the earlier seating being reserved for residents who were in wheelchairs or had walkers and needed special assistance with their food trays). My Mom also loved the cafeteria style setup where residents could pick out whatever they desired in entrées, vegetables, salads, and desserts. My Mom, a dessert-lover, was in heaven. Each time I walked through the line my Mom was so excited, introducing me to all of the workers behind the counter, even if I had met them before. Then one evening, I showed up for dinner without calling her beforehand. She was thrilled to see me, but also seemed a little rattled. She was running around her small studio apartment looking for the guest tickets, which were required before I could go to dinner with her. She found them, but she didn't seem like herself as we rode the elevator down to the dining room. When we got downstairs, the first thing I noticed was that she was attempting to enter the exit door of the dining room. I said quickly, "You're going the wrong way", and she said, "Silly me, I don't know what I was thinking."

As we entered the line, one of the workers said, "Hi, Mrs. Woodward, do you want your usual chicken?" My Mom looked around as if Mrs. Woodward wasn't her name. Then she asked, "Do I usually get chicken?" The worker looked startled, for I think my Mom ate chicken every day of her life. Seeing the surprised look on the worker's face, she quickly said, "Yes, my usual chicken is fine, and please give my daughter whatever she wants." My Mom barely ate her dinner that night. In retrospect I wonder if she was feeling lost for the first time, as she had forgotten where the entrance was, her name, and her customary dinner fare. I didn't do what I should have done that night, which was to comfort her because I didn't know what she needed. She looked confused, but rather than address it, I continued with my usual dinner-time chatter.

One of the few things my Mom had become passionate about was Tai Chi. She began taking classes around the year 2000 not long after moving into Friendship Terrace. I don't believe I'd ever seen my Mom that committed to an activity. She became easy to shop for on holidays and birthdays. Renee and I simply got her a new Tai Chi book or DVD. My Mom prided herself on getting to the class early to set up the chairs and to provide any assistance the instructor needed, including helping other class members. She looked forward to the Tuesday and Thursday classes and never would schedule any other activity on those days. Then one Tuesday I called to see how the class had gone. My Mom paused for a minute, and then said, "I was so busy today that I forgot it was

Tuesday". I could tell by her voice that she was stunned that she had neglected to attend her favorite activity, something she would never intentionally miss, and which took place right down the hall from her apartment. She then said, "I'll be putting reminders up on the refrigerator so I won't ever forget again." I could tell she was exasperated with herself for her forgetfulness. I tried to reassure her, saying, "Oh I'm sure you'll be there bright and early on Thursday." I too was a little worried, but I couldn't think of what to do at that moment. To my knowledge, my Mom never missed another class.

In January of 2006 my Mom lost her way in Washington, DC's Providence Hospital. Although hospitals are large facilities, making it an easy thing to get lost, Providence was a place that my mother knew like the back of her hand. She had been going there for most of her adult life for routine doctor's appointments and lab work. For many years, she also had taken my grandmother there for her appointments too.

Now, in spite of the fact that I now was accompanying her to doctor's appointments, I didn't want her to think I was taking away all of her independence. When her appointment was finished, my Mom wanted to go to the rest room before the forty minute trip home. Perhaps she was a little frustrated about my new role of escorting her almost everywhere because she said, "I want to go to the bathroom by myself. I'll come right back." As it was winter, I stayed in the waiting area holding our coats and purses. I remember looking at the clock, but I don't know exactly why. In seven minutes when my Mom hadn't returned, I began to squirm in my seat, trying not to be too worried. At ten minutes, I stood up and looked around the area for my Mom. I realized that I was sitting behind a wall, so when my Mom came out of the restroom she would not have been able to see me unless she remembered exactly where I was sitting.

My stomach immediately began churning. I went into the restroom, but all the stalls were empty and there was no sign of her. I went around the floor and back to the lab where we had done the blood work. My biggest fear was that if my Mom hadn't remembered where I was sitting, maybe she would think that she had come to the hospital alone. That could have meant that she had left the hospital and had gotten on a bus, which is how she had traveled to the hospital for more than thirty years. I ran as fast as I could to the lobby and out to the bus stop. To my chagrin, there was a bus pulling off as I got there. My mind was racing. Was my Mom on that bus? I was terrified that I was going to have to submit her photo to show on the news announcing that she was missing! I ran into Judith Davis, a priest and a friend of mine who was there with her son Jamie. I told her that I had lost my Mom. I felt like a frightened parent who had lost her child. I had never been that scared, nor have I been that scared since. After Judith promised to pray for a great outcome, I headed to the elevator to go back upstairs to where I last saw my Mom.

Then the most amazing thing happened. I saw her walking toward me with a hospital security officer. My Mom pointed to me and said to the officer, "There's my daughter right there." I ran to her, hugging her as hard as I could, and I thanked the officer. He told me that my Mom approached him, saying, "I can't find my daughter." My Mom remembered that I had been a security professional for more than twenty years and decided that if she could find a security officer that person could help her to locate me again. That wonderful officer kept my Mom calm and focused by asking her why she had come to the hospital that day. She told him, "To do blood work in the lab." He then took my Mom back to the lab to search for me. He told me that when my Mom came out of the restroom, she had gotten on the elevator instead of walking straight ahead to where I was sitting. She ended up two floors above where she needed to be and walked around for ten minutes alone before asking for help. I was so grateful for him reuniting me with my Mom that I wrote a letter of thanks to his manager and the hospital director. His kindness kept my Mom's anxiety at bay. I learned later that the hospital had procedures for lost children, and adults with memory challenges. I was most impressed and incredibly grateful.

After my Mom got lost at the hospital, it became clear that something was going on with her. I decided to make an appointment with her family doctor so we could determine what that "something" was. Her doctor is a very popular physician. His patients love him, which is a great thing because they also have to wait hours to see him. I have lots of patience, but firmly believe that when you have a medical appointment, you should be seen within 15 minutes of the scheduled time. In the case of my Mom's doctor, it's more like three hours. If my Mom hadn't loved her doctor, I would have refused to take her and would have found a physician more respectful of his patient's time. On the day that I escorted my Mom to her appointment, I had a list of questions I wanted to ask the doctor. She was scheduled to see him at 11:00 a.m. We arrived at 10:45 a.m., yet we didn't get in to see the doctor until 3:40 p.m. I started to leave several times. Although waiting wasn't unusual, the delay of this particular this day was the longest ever. He is a fine doctor, but no one is worth that long a wait. By the time we got in to see him, I was so upset that I never asked him my series of questions.

I did ask about the signs for Alzheimer's disease. He told me that he could administer a short test, but that he was sure she didn't have Alzheimer's, for, as he had known her for thirty years, he would have noticed it by now. Huh? What did he mean? How could he notice anything when he always was hours behind in seeing his patients, and then, when he did see them, he would spend an average of a few minutes with them? He asked my Mom a few questions, at the end of which he proclaimed that my Mom didn't have Alzheimer's disease. It was more than likely, he thought, that she had the beginnings of dementia. He then encouraged me to make an appointment with the neurologist down the hall. That's when I should have said, "That's OK, I'll find my own neurologist." But I replied that I would follow his direction. I tried to downplay my aggravation with him, but as it was 4:30 in the afternoon, I felt as if we had wasted the entire day. One of the doctor's nurses had been with him for almost all of my adult life, and as we left the office she said, "Nothing ever changes around here. I'm sorry for the long wait". At that moment, with a staff member apologizing for the doctor's behavior, I decided that my Mom and I would not be returning.

I made an appointment for my Mom with the recommended neurologist, but I didn't like him at all. I found him to be patronizing, talking down to us. Moreover, he didn't seem really interested in my Mom or her care. He spent about ten minutes with us, delivering his findings in a dispassionate, fact-of-the matter tone.

"You have a very mild case of dementia," he said, "but it will get worse." My Mom asked, "Am I going to die soon?" The doctor replied, "No, you're just going to need to take medicine for it." My Mom said, "I already take two pills. I don't want to take anything else." "You don't have a choice," was the doctor's response, his voice steely and unfeeling. I was angry, but only said, "She doesn't have to do anything she doesn't want to." "She does," he said, "if you want her to remember you and live a fairly normal life." I wanted so badly to slap him, and then to offer him a free spot in my communications class! I felt that he needed serious improvement in his physician-patient interactions *and* an attitude adjustment.

Aricept was prescribed for my Mom. She was very reluctant to take it, but I believe that she, raised to believe that doctors know best, felt intimidated by the neurologist and gave in to his recommendation. She diligently began taking the drug although she hated how it made her feel. She had horrible nightmares and was very tired all the time. As the doctor clearly had stated that the drug wouldn't help my Mom to get any better, but that it might stop the progression of the disease, I told her that she didn't have to continue taking the drug. But being the obedient soul that she is, she said she would try it for a little longer to see if the side effects lessened in intensity.

We were told that the typical side effects of Aricept were diarrhea, dizziness, loss of appetite, muscle cramps, nausea, fatigue, insomnia, and vomiting. I explained all of this to my Mom, as best I could seeking to prepare her for whatever might arise. In the fine print of the pharmaceutical literature there was mention of some less common side effects, hallucinations and pacing, both of which my Mom experienced as soon as she began to take the drug. Early one morning before 7:30 a.m., she called. (I already had arisen and was fully into the responsibilities of my day. As my Mom had never been a top-of-the-morning person, I was surprised, even alarmed to see her number appear on the caller ID.) Quickly, I answered, immediately hearing the panic in her voice. "That medicine is giving me hallucinations." she said. I had not told her about the potential of that side effect, so I was amazed that as she'd never had deliria, she made the connection that the Aricept, the only new thing in her life, must have been the cause. I asked her to describe the hallucinations. She spoke of a horrible dream in which my dead grandparents were wearing masks and chasing her, and then many other of our departed relatives also escaped from their graves and began to pursue her. Her account frightened me too. She also mentioned that she was pacing around her small apartment, something she never had done. I called the doctor's office. Though he spoke to me, he manifested the same distance and disinterest as I had experienced of him when in his office. He assured me that the side effects would diminish as time went on, and most likely would go away. He did advise that if I wanted to change my Mom's drug, we could discuss it at my next appointment which was six months away. Was he kidding? He may have been ok with the possibility that my Mom could have hallucinations for the next six months, but I certainly wasn't. However, his response was fine with me because I already had planned to find a new doctor.

In May of 2006, my Mom experienced the ultimate Aricept side effect, and it was a bad dream in and of itself. My Mom had a doctor's appointment with her gastroenterologist to get the results of her colonoscopy she'd had two weeks prior. As I now accompanied my Mom into the exam rooms, I got her situated on the exam table as we waited for the doctor. The doctor had informed us that he would be a few minutes late because he needed to take an important phone call. While we sat, my Mom said she felt dizzy and I suggested she lay back on the table instead of sitting up straight. We had been playing a memory game with her grocery list. She was doing a great job recalling the list of items. All of a sudden she stopped talking. At first, I wasn't worried because I thought she was simply trying to remember another item from her list. But when I called her name, she didn't answer. Her eyes and mouth were open and she was staring straight ahead. She wasn't breathing and I felt no pulse. I threw open the door to the exam room and yelled for help. The doctor came running. He instantly called a Code Blue. As his office was attached to the Washington Hospital Center, medical personnel came running from everywhere. Two of them jumped on my Mom's gurney and began CPR while six others ran alongside holding tubes and an IV. It felt as if I was watching an episode of a television medical show. What was happening? We had come to get some test results. Why was my Mom now on her way to the emergency room in cardiac arrest?

I was beside myself with fear however they were able to revive my Mom. While she waited in the ER for a regular hospital bed to become available, her neurologist walked by to see one of his patients who also was in the ER. I immediately jumped up and hurriedly explained to him what had happened. Still, much to my shock, he seemed uninterested, saying, "I have a mental health emergency right now that I have to get to, but I'll come back and talk to you later." I acted as if I didn't hear him, for my Mom's circumstances also constituted an emergency. I asked him if the Aricept could have caused this as I heard one of the ER physicians mention the drug as a potential cause of her heart stoppage. My question appeared to anger him. "I don't know why they said that! We can't possibly know that yet! I only deal in facts!" With that, he walked away. I was furious, wondering if there was someone, *anyone* to whom I could report this jerk of a doctor. I also felt helpless, able to do nothing, but only to wait. I contacted my sister Renee in California who assumed my call was about our Aunt Diane, now in her third month of her cancer diagnosis. I also talked to Diane who now for the most part was spending her days in bed. I sat alone in the ER as both Tim and Kim were working. Both Renee and Diane apologized for not being able to be of any help. We all thought this may be an ominous sign of what was to come.

After a week of testing in the hospital, the doctors determined that it indeed was the Aricept that had stopped my Mom's heart. She already was taking a heart medicine for a rapid heartbeat, so Aricept never should have been prescribed. I was told that as all of the dementia drugs are from the same family, my Mom was going to have to live with the progression of the disease without the assistance of any drug therapies. She wasn't upset by that at all as she hated having to take the drug. I was relieved in a sense because I knew she wouldn't have any more hallucinations, but I was also afraid because I didn't have any idea of how fast the disease would progress.

My Mom's primary doctor pointed out that on that fateful day had I not been in the exam room she would have been dead by the time the doctor had finished his phone call. So, in an ironic twist, my Mom having dementia allowed me to save her life. Funny thing. That incident had scared the gastroenterologist so badly that we never saw him again *and* I never received the results from her colonoscopy!

The little things had added up to a really big thing...but my Mom recovered nicely from her traumatic health event and doesn't remember it at all.

Things went along nicely for the next year or so. The disease didn't seem to be progress much at all. To celebrate our 23rd anniversary in the spring of 2007, Tim and I went to Europe for three weeks. My cousin JoAnne promised to keep an eye on my Mom while I was gone. I had purchased enough groceries and then some to last the entire time I'd be gone. My Mom's favorite breakfast meal was oatmeal, which she ate almost every day. Prior to my departure, my Mom had one half-full box and an unopened box of oatmeal. Still, to be on the safe side I brought an additional box. Talking to JoAnne following the wonderful trip, she told me that she had gone to the Safeway to buy oatmeal for my Mom. Given the abundant supply on hand, I was surprised, even shocked. JoAnne told me that she had looked through my Mom's cabinets before going to the store and there was no oatmeal. I kept asking myself, and then my Mom, "What happened to that oatmeal?" Her answer was that she had eaten it all. It didn't understand it at the time, but later it would definitely make sense.

In 2008, my Mom forgot to keep her appointment to get her taxes done, which was provided free of charge for all the residents in her apartment building. My Mom always was on top of her tax preparation and, like many people, she kept all the previous year's receipts and related materials in different colored folders. Each year when the management staff gave my Mom her appointment time she would share the date with me, and then at least a week ahead of time gather her forms and W-2's in a folder. As the 2008 tax season approached, I asked my Mom when the tax preparation folks would be coming that year. She said that she didn't remember, but that she did recall receiving the notice under her door several weeks earlier. She said she'd call the management office and let me know.

A few days later, my Mom called to say that she had forgotten that she'd already been given an appointment time and that the office had reminded her of the date. She seemed embarrassed that she hadn't recalled her appointment time and had to contact the office. I told her not to worry, for I was sure that she wasn't the first person to do that. My Mom said, "Well it's ok now; because I have the appointment on my calendar and on the refrigerator." I put the date on my calendar too.

The day of my Mom's appointment, I was surprised that I didn't get a call from her that the taxes were done. I was busy at work, so I called her the next day. When I asked her how everything had gone, there was a long pause on the other end of the phone. She said, "I don't think it was time for my appointment yet." I paused too, and then said, "Your appointment was yesterday". Then came another long pause. Here again was another occasion for my surprise, for my Mom would never forget any free service available to her.

She was mortified, so I said, "Don't worry. I'll call and see if I can get you another appointment." I wouldn't dare ask my Mom to call the office again, and she seemed so relieved that I was going to take care of it. As her sponsor, I could call any time to get information or ask questions about the services provided in the building. When I made the call, I was informed that no more tax preparation appointments were available. I also learned that my Mom had missed *two* appointments, and, because of that, other residents had not been able to take advantage of the free tax services. Additionally, we were to be charged a service fee! My heart sank, but I told the office administrator that I would immediately pay the service charge. I didn't tell my Mom about the penalty as she already was upset enough and I wanted to spare her feelings. At that moment, I decided to get more involved in my Mom's day to day life. I took her tax folders to the H&R Block office in my neighborhood and paid to have her taxes done. I told her that I had found another "free" service because I wanted her to be able to move on from this event. I "fixed" the situation by getting my Mom's taxes done, but I didn't, *couldn't* fix the cause of my Mom's worsening condition.

At around the same time, another significant issue arose when my Mom thought all of her money had been removed from her checking and money market accounts because she had missed a bank deadline. She, distraught, had called to say that I needed to come over right away because she had something to tell me. When I arrived, I found her nearly hysterical. Talking much faster than normal, she explained that she had received a letter from the bank stating that she needed to call them prior to a certain date or all her funds would be relinquished to the bank. I knew that couldn't be possible, but I couldn't calm her down and she could no longer find the letter. So, I decided that we needed to go to the bank, so that my Mom could "see" that her money was still there.

We got in line and thankfully had a very nice young man to help us. He confirmed what I had suspected, that the letter my Mom had received was simply an announcement that new features were now available for savings and money market accounts, and that taking advantage of the features required response by a certain date. The bank representative, recognizing that my Mom was a little confused, was very empathetic toward her, trying his best to explain that her money was not lost, but secure in spite of her having "ignored" the letter. She wasn't satisfied, so I asked him if he would turn his computer screen around so that my Mom could "see" that her money was still there. I am a visual person. So, too, is my Mom who, when assured that her money was still in her account, smiled. I was relieved, but also wondered how many more situations like this were in our future.

The final straw came one month when my Mom forgot to pay her rent. As her sponsor, I received a late notice and a penalty fee. I don't think my Mom, who believed that a delinquent payment, even once, resulted in bad credit, had ever paid anything late in her life. (This is one anxiety I did inherit from my Mom, for I'm terrified of paying anything late.) To prevent this from happening again, I set up an automatic payment from my Mom's bank account.

At this point it became painfully clear that the things occurring with my Mom were no longer "little things" and that it was time for me to accept the fact that this disease "is what it is" and required more action on my part.

Chapter III – It Is What It Is

At some point the truth about this disease, that it takes away your loved one's ability to be independent, actually hits you. When that realization comes, you can't make excuses any more. That reality dawned for me in the middle of 2009 when my Mom recounted two incidents that occurred in her building, both of which she attributed to her being an African-American.

I was more than stunned by her claim! My Mom loved her retirement community and never had mentioned any kind of racial incident even though there were relatively few African-American residents in a building of several hundred apartments.

I asked my Mom to explain exactly what happened. She told me that she had gone to the basement laundry room, placed her clothes in the washer, and then returned to her apartment to do other things. Later, she put the clothes in the dryer and looked at the time so she would know when to come back to fold her clothes. Although she had forgotten to go back as soon as the dryer would have stopped, she did return to the laundry room within an hour of her clothes being done, only to discover that her garments were missing. She waited in the laundry room for about fifteen minutes to see if the person who had removed her clothes would return them.

When no one appeared, she went to the front desk to report that someone had taken her clothes. She was told that a sign would be posted with her name and apartment number requesting that the laundry be returned. She was also assured that whatever happened had been unintentional. However, my Mom didn't believe that her laundry would be brought back to her. Rather, she was convinced that her laundry was taken by someone who knew it belonged to an African-American and that her belongings had been thrown away. I asked her whether she had had any problems with anyone in the building or knew of anyone who would do such a thing. She didn't know who had done it, nevertheless she was sure that it had been deliberate. She wanted to file a complaint and asked me if I would accompany her to a meeting with the director of the retirement community so we could get to the bottom of this. I assured her that I would, but told her I first wanted to gather more information. I guess my answer didn't please her, for she yelled, "You don't believe me!" I told her that it wasn't that I didn't believe her, but that as a security professional experienced with conducting investigations, I wanted to ensure that I had all of the facts. Although she was unhappy about it, she agreed that we could wait to make the appointment with the director.

During the same conversation, my Mom also reported that she was being forced out of the Stretch and Flex class that she loved. This was unbelievable to me, but I listened to what she shared. My Mom had a great role as a class participant, reporting early to each session, putting the chairs in a circle, and placing the hand weights next to everyone's chair. Every year, she received an award for arranging the room and assisting the instructor. While my Mom didn't love Stretch and Flex as much as she did Tai Chi, she never wanted to miss the class.

My Mom told me that she had gone to the exercise room on the day and time of the class, but no one was there. She went to the front desk seeking an explanation and was told that the class had been changed to a different day and time for that week. My Mom, not knowing about the schedule shift, was hurt. The person at the desk told her that all class members had received notes under their doors announcing the temporary change. My Mom insisted that she had not gotten such word *and* that she unfairly and intentionally had been excluded. The desk person promised that someone would get back to her about why she hadn't been informed, but insisted that the oversight had not been intended.

The stories of these incidents presented me with quite the dilemma. I loved this retirement community as did my Mom, so I needed to find the best way to approach this. I didn't want to doubt my Mom because she was so convinced that these situations had occurred. Yet she had lived in this community for ten years and never had had any problems at all, much less racial in nature.

Having in mind my Mom's descriptions of her missing clothing, I initiated my own little investigation. There was a laundry and folding service available for residents in the building that included picking up, washing, folding, and returning the laundry to the residents. I checked with the service to confirm what I already knew. My Mom never had used that service. I returned to my Mom's apartment and asked her to tell me again exactly what was missing. As she described one of the items, looking in her closet, I saw it neatly folded on a shelf. Taking the garment in hand, I said, "This looks like the one that's missing!" My Mom responded excitedly, "That *is* the one that was missing! Who gave it to you?" I told her that it was on the shelf where I was standing and that no one had returned it to me. "That's so strange," she said, "I wonder who put that in there?" I asked her to come with me and look. One by one we found all of the missing clothing. At once she was shocked, confused, and embarrassed. I concluded that my Mom simply had forgotten that she had returned to the laundry room to retrieve her clothes folded them and put them away in the closet as usual. As kindly as I could I said, "Well I think you just don't remember that you picked up your laundry and brought it back here." Her head dropped and she said, "I have to do better with my memory". I couldn't bring myself to recount for her that she had accused another resident of a racial slight in taking her clothes.

Searching for the note about the exercise class, I looked through the stack of papers on my Mom's kitchen table, not finding it. I spoke to the person who had distributed the flyers asking whether she placed one under my Mom's door. She was "positive," she said, that she had done so. She remembered, she also told me, because my Mom's apartment was right down the hall from the exercise room *and*, more importantly, because my Mom was the most important person in the class, they definitely needed her to know. The lady also relayed to me that she distributed the flyers in the early morning. When arriving at my Mom's door she could hear the sound of running water and thought maybe my Mom was preparing breakfast. "Hmmm," I thought to myself. I went to my Mom's kitchen cabinets, and lo and behold, there I found the flyer. I called my Mom over to the cabinets. "What's that?" I asked. My Mom, retrieving the paper from amidst the plates and cups, said "Look, it's the flyer, I wonder why they put it up there?" As calmly and as lovingly as I could I told her the likely scenario was that after she had gotten the note from under her door, she read it in the kitchen area and placed it in the cabinet and forgot. She didn't recall any of that. She said, "I don't know why I wouldn't remember that". I suggested that it would probably be a good idea for her to apologize to everyone she had accused of not advising her about the change. I was thrilled that I had discovered what had happened and we had dodged that bullet of my Mom's unfounded accusations. However, believing that this situation could happen and, in all likelihood, *would* happen again, when I got home I told Tim that it may be time to look for another place for my Mom where another level of care was available.

My Mom was aware of how much our relationship had changed, that I now was accompanying her to nearly every appointment, speaking on her behalf and making most of the important decisions. I tried to grant her a few moments of independence whenever I could. She was not happy about losing her sense of personal liberty, but she tolerated it. I knew I needed to take a harder line after the incidents of missing the tax prep appointment and failing to pay the rent. I also determined that I needed to take over my Mom's checkbook *and* that I'd have to be firm with her because she wasn't going to like my decision. I have learned that these kinds of circumstances, involving direct and careful speech, require the right timing and the right words. I found it very helpful to write down what I wanted to say, and then practice before delivering it. Rehearsing beforehand helps in case the meeting becomes emotional (as it is likely to be). It's important to push through the emotion and get to what needs to be said. I wasn't exactly sure how much additional care my

Mom needed, but I was sure that she and her money would be vulnerable to con artists. Thus, removing her control of her checkbook would be a difficult decision, but one made necessary in an effort to protect her assets.

As I took more responsibility for my Mom and, thus more independence from her, I sought to put myself in her place recognizing how she might have felt. I took that opportunity to buy my Mom a Personal Expressions card. At times, I find that someone else's words can express more clearly and profoundly what you want to say to a loved one.

Because of my Mom's dementia, I wanted to get a card that she could read repeatedly so to be reminded of how I felt about her and what I was attempting to do, even and especially when we were not together.

The words of the card were as follows...

> *"All of us have moments when we look at our lives and ask "How did I get here?" Living is so full of unpredictable twists – sometimes it's hard to keep up, adjusting ourselves to the life we have while letting go of the life we planned.*

> *I think you may be experiencing some of that now...when some days are better than others and nothing seems as certain as it used to be. Just be sure to be good to yourself right now. Give yourself time to rest, to reflect, to start to heal...and know that anytime you need someone to talk with, I'm here for you.* K.A. Moon

I loved these sentiments, for they captured everything I thought my Mom may have been feeling. On the inside of the card I wrote:

Dear Mom,

Please read this card when you are feeling down and always remember...

> 1) *I have your best interest at heart*
> 2) *I would never do anything to hurt you*
> 3) *I won't force you to do anything*
> 4) *I love you more than anything...*

Love, Loretta

My Mom still has the card, and I know she reads it quite often. I hope that she still understands the meaning of every word and can always feel my love and support for her.

In addition to cards and other types of emotional support you can offer to your loved one, there also are a number of steps that may need to be taken to deal head on with the events that are occurring so to protect your loved one from harm.

Following, I share some advice, drawn from the research I have conducted, the steps I have taken, and the lessons I've learned thus far.

1) Investigate all community, county, state, and federal resources available to you and your loved one. Keep copies of all paperwork as well as the names and phone numbers of anyone you contact regarding programs and services. Every state has different rules and regulations

on eligibility, so be sure to research thoroughly every avenue you are considering.

In my Mom's retirement community, the rent was quite affordable, especially for retirees with adequate pensions. My Mom's retirement income was modest, all of it consumed by her monthly rent. In 1999, she applied and was accepted into the reduced rent program, lowering her rent in half. This allowed her to pay for her other necessities such as prescriptions, groceries, and clothing. Each year we had to re-apply for the reduced rent, but it was more than worth it. In the application process, we were required to supply bank statements, out of pocket insurance expenses and prescription costs, annual grocery costs, and all other expenses. After the examination of her personal documents, her monthly rent was determined. I made the gathering of my Mom's documents a game for the two of us and it worked well. She liked making a list and checking everything off the list that we needed. Including her in the process built her self-esteem.

Now that my Mom lives in a different place, obtaining a negotiated or reduced rent wasn't possible. However, she is assessed the lowest rate because she still can take care of her personal hygiene, bathe, and dress herself. As her current care costs are more than her retirement income, it didn't take long, actually, within two years to deplete her savings. Like many children, I now subsidize my Mom's care. Trying to think ahead, I called the county in which I live and asked about the availability of assistance services. Following the counsel I received, I got my Mom on a three-year waiting list for a Medicare-type payment plan through which her caregiver's business would receive a monthly disbursement based on her income that

I hoped would be accepted as full compensation for her care. In retrospect, I also wish that I had thought ahead and investigated what financial services may have been available a year before my Mom's savings were depleted. Alas, you live and learn.

2) Ensure that powers of attorneys, both medical and financial, a living will, and a will have been drafted, signed, and ratified. If a power of attorney isn't accepted in your jurisdiction, guardianship may be necessary.

Power of attorney is the name given to the person or persons who are appointed to make decisions for those who, due to accident, illness, or age, are unable to continue to care for themselves. A partner, an adult child, or a friend can serve as power of attorney as long as they are trustworthy and willing to act on your loved one's behalf. When there are disagreements within the family as to who should serve in this capacity, an impartial power of attorney from a trust company can be an acceptable alternative.

Without a power of attorney, no one can sign legal documents or checks for your loved one, potentially leaving bills unpaid.

It isn't mandatory to enlist professional legal services to draft a power of attorney. Free documents can be downloaded from the internet and can be signed at a bank or by a notary public. If possible, have a professional review your paperwork to ensure that everything is clear and nothing has been omitted. Keep in mind that a power of attorney is a powerful document and gives permission for someone else to do whatever your loved one could do. Unlimited power can be given or it can be restricted to financial matters, property matters, or health matters. It also is important to know that a power of attorney is void upon your loved one's death.

In our case, in November 2009, I hired a lawyer who helped me with a power of attorney for my Mom. Word for word, I read the document to my Mom, asking her questions to confirm that she understood every stipulation before she signed it. My lawyer suggested that I ask her several questions, even if she didn't understand it all, in the future event that I would need to become her guardian. If guardianship was necessary, a judge would be obliged to ask my Mom a series of questions to determine that I was not taking advantage of her.

I found it interesting that my Mom's bank didn't recognize her power of attorney. I learned that many banks now require guardianship because it is believed that it reduces the potential for fraud that can occur with powers of attorney. Thankfully, years ago my Mom had added the names of my sister and me on her bank account. That spared me a lot of work to gain access to her funds. I'm guessing that, at some point, I will have to become my Mom's guardian.

Living Wills

While a power of attorney delineates the duties for your loved one's finances, personal property, and medical care, a living will addresses the provision of medical care in the urgent circumstances at the end of life, outlining desired and undesired life-support measures.

In some jurisdictions, living wills do not have full legal status, so be sure you investigate fully the relevant statutes and ordinances. Without a living will, life and death decisions concerning your loved one could be made by medical professionals.

My Mom has had a living will since well before she was diagnosed with dementia. I was still in my twenties when she had a neighbor and me sign her living will. Thus, when the time comes, I intend to follow her instructions to the letter, which, blessedly will relieve a great deal of pressure for me to make a choice I may not be prepared to make.

Conservatorship/Guardianship

Conservatorship and adult guardianship basically mean the same thing, as states typically use one name or the other. Conservatorship is used when an individual can't make important personal decisions. A judge then will appoint someone, called the "conservator" or "guardian" to make those determinations. Such decisions have the legal backing of the court and can involve your loved ones finances, medical, and personal care. As in the case of anything else, there are advantages and disadvantages to conservatorship, which I list below.

Advantages

- Family members know that someone is making decisions
- Legal authority is established for dealing with third parties

- A process is provided for a judge to approve major decisions

Disadvantages

- Costly to set up, requiring a lawyer, legal documentation, and a court hearing
- Time-consuming, including extensive ongoing paperwork
- Potentially humiliating for an older adult who is still somewhat capable of making decisions
- Can be emotionally draining when family members disagree about who the conservator should be.

Two things are necessary to make a conservatorship appropriate. First, the person must be physically or mentally incapable of making important personal decisions. Secondly, your loved one doesn't already have legal documents (e.g., a living will and power of attorney for finances) that cover decisions about personal and financial matters.

- If there is no power of attorney for finances, a conservator of the estate is required. If there is no medical directive or living will, a conservator could make any necessary healthcare decisions.

- Even if there is a medical directive, a conservator may still be needed to decide health matters that aren't covered in the medical directive. Even if there is a power of attorney for medical and financial concerns, a conservator still may be needed to make decisions about your loved one's living, for example, place of residence.

I have all the paperwork I need to begin the process for becoming my Mom's guardian if that need arises in the future.

3) Ensure that your loved one has a social worker, if required (many states mandate this, especially if your loved one has a designated conservator).

Social workers can be state-appointed if the loved one will be going through the conservator process. The social worker will be the family's advocate throughout the process, which culminates in a competency hearing before a judge. If your loved one is adjudged incompetent, the court will appoint a family member as legal guardian. When no family member is willing or able to serve in this capacity, the court will appoint a legal guardian, usually a social worker who will work directly with your loved one, offering counseling and aid, as frequently as needed, and contacting other individuals who are involved. The social worker will maintain telephone contacts with the loved one's caregivers regarding care, activities, services, and treatment, and will attend conferences and treatment planning meetings with caregivers and other medical and mental health providers.

Although I don't need one immediately, I have interviewed two social workers from the county where I live in Maryland so that I know what to expect when the time comes. I found it to be a very useful experience. Moreover, the two people I met were simply fabulous, providing a wealth of information and, as importantly, taking the fear out of the process for me. I felt uncomfortable that the process would end with my Mom being declared "incompetent", but they, in their careful and caring counsel, allowed me to relinquish the negative stigma that I had associated with the process.

4) Have an initial family meeting to bring everyone up to speed on the loved one's situation, and determine if follow up meetings are necessary to keep everyone in the loop.

A family meeting wasn't necessary to discuss my Mom. I did tell my sister Renee, my Aunt Frannie and my Mom's friend Mrs. Adams of my plans. It was a comfort and support to me that they agreed with everything I intended to do concerning my Mom's care. After all the decisions were made, I also informed my Uncle Donald, my Mom's brother. He also was in agreement with the plans. Although he hasn't been that involved in our lives, I still felt obligated to share the news with him.

Happily, my situation concerning the notification of family members was easy. I am aware of the difficult circumstances encountered by friends who have engaged in painful battles with relatives over what care is best for their loved one. There have been instances where relatives have stopped speaking to one another over disagreements about care and, particularly, the dissolution of property. In my research, I learned that there are elder care mediation services available online when resolution isn't possible among family members.

5) Ensure that your loved one's medical team provides the level and quality of care that is needed and is willing to work with the family.

I learned this lesson the hard way. I failed to take action quickly enough to replace my Mom's neurologist in spite of what I perceived as his lack of care, often manifesting itself in his impersonal, intimidating, and patronizing manner. I wanted a doctor who was competent and who, with kindness, would treat my Mom with the respect and dignity she deserved as a human being.

As fate *and luck* would have it, the neurologist disqualified himself from my Mom's care. I received a call from his office saying that the doctor had multiple sclerosis and was physically unable to continue his neurology practice. As my sister also had MS, and I was familiar with the progression of her disease, I was surprised to learn of the doctor's diagnosis as I never saw in him any evidence of debilitating symptoms. I was sorry that he was ill, *but* relieved we wouldn't have to see him again.

Now, as he was a member of a large team of DC neurologists, I was told to select another physician from that group. When I called, I spoke with the best appointment scheduler in America! Without uttering a negative word about my Mom's previous doctor, he suggested that I select the female neurologist of the practice who specialized in care for the elderly with dementia and Alzheimer's. With confidence, he said that I would "love her" as she was vastly different from my Mom's previous doctor. Taking his recommendation, I made an appointment with Dr. Catherine Coerver. From the moment she walked into the exam room, I knew that she was the doctor for us. I say "us" because my Mom and I are a team when it comes to her care. While I do make the important decisions, I involve her at each stage and at every step of our journey too. I never want her to think that I disrespect or disregard her in any way.

What I love about Dr. Coerver is that whenever she appears, she greets my Mom as if they are old friends. They have a conversation and then she asks my Mom a series of questions to check the progression of her dementia. My Mom doesn't answer any of the questions correctly – such as the date of the day or the season of the year or her address. In spite of this Dr. Coerver always is encouraging. If its spring and my Mom guesses that it's summer, she'll say, "Not quite. When do the flowers bloom?" and my Mom enthusiastically will say, "Spring!" Then, as if my Mom had won the lottery, Dr. Coerver will exclaim, "Right! Great job!" My Mom then smiles broadly. I love how this doctor makes my Mom feel special.

After they finish their conversation and the questions, Dr. Coerver then asks my Mom for her "permission" to make some inquiries of me. My Mom always gives her consent. I LOVE that! I never correct anything my Mom says during her own "talk time" with the doctor. I wait until it's my turn and then share everything that is going on with my Mom. After the very first visit with Dr. Coerver, I called the appointment scheduler to thank him for his suggestion. I feel so comfortable with her and totally trust her care of and plan for my Mom.

I've also decided against continuing to see my Mom's general practitioner for whom we would wait for hours. The same goes for her endocrinologist who she used to like, but no longer remembers. I have replaced them with one rheumatologist, who also is my doctor. My Mom loves him as do I. He is young and energetic and he too makes my Mom feel special. As a rheumatologist, he can prescribe both her thyroid medicine and her Reclast infusion for her osteoporosis. I not only appreciate that we now have a "one-stop shop" for my Mom's care very close to where we live, but also that it is so beneficial for her state of mind. She's neither intimidated nor made to feel anxious by either doctor she is seeing now. It doesn't get *any* better than that. No matter what the future holds for us, I feel great about this new team going forward.

Chapter IV – Just Do It!

When it becomes obvious that a decision must be made, make it quickly. As the commercial says, just do it! Making hard choices can be painful, but facing them, seeking the counsel of others, and weighing your options will help you to get through them. Prolonging the making of definitive decisions not only extends and deepens the hurt and pain, it also can jeopardize the safety of your loved one.

The end to my Mom's living alone without oversight came fairly swiftly. As a security person, I had checked into the ADT system called Pulse, which allows family members to monitor the loved one via camera and if need be, to call for help. I had made an appointment with an ADT representative to learn more about how the system could work for my Mom, but that plan all changed in one day.

On a September afternoon in 2009, I arrived at my Mom's apartment building with items I'd purchased for her. When I got to the elevator one of the women who lived on my Mom's floor (who for the purposes of recounting this incident I shall name "Mary") asked me if I was Doris's daughter. I nodded affirmatively. She said, "Come sit down. I need to talk to you for a few minutes". She asked me whether anyone from the office management had called me about my Mom in the last couple of weeks. I answered no. "I didn't think so," she said, "or you would have been here by now". I immediately got a sinking feeling.

Mary began by telling me that my Mom had been having some problems over the last several days. She had observed my Mom throwing items into the incinerator that clearly were not trash, including unopened packs of cookies, boxes of crackers, and containers of applesauce. When Mary called my Mom's name and asked why she was throwing the new items away, my Mom replied that those items didn't belong to her and because she didn't know who had brought them, she didn't want to eat them and, therefore, was throwing them away. When Mary explained to my Mom that I had brought the items for her, my Mom told her that as I hadn't visited lately, the items couldn't have come from me and must have been delivered to her apartment by mistake. Mary then told my Mom that she would have the front desk call me so I could come and check on her, which she did. However, no one called me. The more Mary talked, the angrier I became.

The story got worse. Mary also shared that earlier in the same week my Mom had come down for dinner, but instead of immediately returning to her apartment after dinner, as was her norm, she sat on the bench outside of the dining room. When Mary asked her what she was doing, my Mom replied that she was resting. Mary later learned that the real reason my Mom hadn't left the dining room area was because she couldn't remember her apartment number or location. Once she confessed her predicament, Mary took my Mom to her apartment and told her that she'd have the front desk to call me and alert me to my mother's increasing difficulties. Listening to Mary, I sat stunned thinking of what I needed to do next. While we talked, one of the dining room employees approached us. Mary said, "This is Ms. Doris's daughter."

She said, "Something is wrong with Ms. Doris. She forgot to come to dinner the last two nights, so I took her dinner to her room". (One of the building rules is that all residents must come to the dining room for dinner unless they are temporarily physically incapacitated. Thus, the dining room employee could have gotten into trouble for taking dinner to my Mom.)

She continued her account that when she arrived at the apartment with dinner, my Mom was still in her pajamas and seemed confused about what time it was. My Mom was surprised to learn that she had missed dinner. The employee told my Mom she would take care of it if she ever missed dinner again. (Customarily, residents were tracked through dining room attendance at which time their names were checked off a list. When, on a given evening, a resident had not informed the management about missing dinner and did not appear, a building representative would be dispatched to the apartment to determine if all was well.) The reason I didn't get a call about my Mom missing dinner more than once in the same week was that the dining room employee, once delivering dinner to my Mom's apartment crossed her off the list as having been "present".

I wish the story had ended there. It didn't. Mary had something more, something worse to tell me. The day before I arrived, Mary went to the front desk to ask if a note had been taken alerting someone to call me about my Mom. No note was found, but assurances were given that I would be contacted. When Mary was asked of the reasons for her concern, she shared the stories she now had told me. The person manning the front desk then relayed to Mary that she, too, had observed something odd with my Mom. In the previous week, my Mom, who

85

usually wore a skirt and blouse, had come to the lobby wearing a business suit accessorized with a pearl necklace and matching earrings. When asked where she was going, my Mom said, "I'm off to work and waiting for my ride". No more questions were asked of my Mom. However, clearly, my Mom, fully retired, wasn't going to work, *and* the person she had mentioned was to pick her up had died years earlier.

On reflection, I don't think I've ever felt as angry about what I consider to be institutional negligence. No one called me about my Mom's behavioral changes. I had received calls about bazaars, bake sales, and other events occurring at the building. I certainly received a call when my Mom failed to pay her rent, however, no one thought or apparently was concerned enough to call me when my Mom began to do things that were out of the ordinary. I realize that this retirement community is a non-assisted living facility, thus the staff is not required to "watch" my Mom. However, I failed to understand then and I cannot understand now how my Mom, passing through the lobby declaring that she was on her way to work, didn't raise the tiniest concern, even suspicion that something was amiss, something requiring, something *deserving* investigation. The long-serving front desk employee knew that my Mom didn't have a job. In retrospect, I suppose I should be grateful that my Mom didn't walk out the front door of the building and potentially become one of those faces you see on a news report of a missing dementia patient.

When Mary had completed her recollections, I felt myself about to cry. I didn't, managing to offer a weak, "Thank you for helping my Mom." As I was still attempting to process all that I had been told, I observed Kathy, a home health care aide, assisting a resident who lived on my Mom's floor. I asked Kathy whether she might be interested in helping my Mom until I could get her moved to another place. As luck would have it, one of the residents Kathy had served was moving to a new home the very next day. Kathy, now with an open space in her schedule, gladly would care for my Mom until I could arrange for new lodging for her, saying, "I love Ms. Doris. I'd love to take care of her." Quickly I wrote her a check for the first three days of work. We agreed that Kathy would arrive at my Mom's apartment in the morning, get her up and moving, fix her breakfast, ensure that she took her medicine, take her to the exercise class, and to dinner, and then to bed at night. We also removed all the burners from the stove so that my Mom could no longer turn on the stove.

I stayed a few hours with Kathy and my Mom to ensure their mutual comfort, although for my Mom's part she seemed at ease with almost anyone.

Now, Kathy also had a story to tell about my Mom. She told me that she had seen my Mom throwing clothes into the incinerator. When she asked my Mom why she was doing that, she told Kathy that the garments weren't hers. Kathy then said that if anything was missing in my Mom's apartment that "cleaning up and cleaning out behavior" likely was the reason why.

I took a quick inventory of the contents of my Mom's closet. Right away, I recognized that four of the five new outfits I had bought for her on our trip to the Lancaster, Pennsylvania, outlet mall were missing. I searched in every drawer and on every shelf to no avail. It struck me that I should not have been surprised. On our return from the mall, my Mom looked at the bags and said, "This isn't mine. Who does this stuff belong to?" Repeatedly, I explained to her that those were her items that we had just purchased to which she responded, "Did I try them on?" I assured that she had and that she looked "simply marvelous" in all the outfits. She replied with a half-convinced, "OK." I should have known that she hadn't accepted a word of what I had said. I now know that the items Kathy saw my Mom throwing away were these very ones that she probably had never worn. Suddenly, mindful that she had also been disposing of food, I was overcome with the possibility that my Mom could also have been discarding important documents.

That evening, following one of the worst visits to my Mom's building, I drove home in rush hour traffic. I was almost in tears, but somehow I felt that I should have seen it all coming and thus, acted much sooner in searching for a new, better equipped residence for my Mom. I remembered that Blanca Plaza, one of my Cha Chas, a dear group of friends who are like sisters, had given me a flyer of a group home for elderly residents called Mamie's Loving Care. The name of the place alone gave me comfort and I smiled for the first time that day.

The next morning, I made two calls first thing. First, to Friendship Terrace to inform the management that, due to my Mom's deteriorating condition, I'd be moving her as soon as I found a new place. The office manager seemed surprised, and asked for specifics regarding the changes in my Mom's behavior. I shared the stories (except for the one about the dining room employee taking my Mom dinner as I didn't want to get her in any trouble). The office manager's only response was, "Oh, I'm sorry." She said she'd let me out of the requirement to give them thirty days' notice of the intention to move. I was grateful for that kindness, but, truth to tell, as I was determined to move my Mom (within an instant, if possible, but certainly in far less time than thirty days!), I willingly would have paid whatever penalty might be assessed.

My second call was to Mamie Young, the owner of Mamie's Loving Care. I told her about my Mom's situation and asked if I could make an appointment to tour her group home. The next day, she met Tim, my Mom, and me and we loved what we saw at both her group homes. Just to ensure I was selecting the best place for my Mom, I visited three other small group homes, but they didn't come close to the warm feeling I received at Ms. Mamie's.

I knew Ms. Mamie's was the right place for my Mom. It is a single family home with three bedrooms upstairs, and a full bath for the residents. The primary caregivers live in the basement. It felt like a family home, and not just a place from which my Mom couldn't escape. Despite the presence of three locks on the front door, installed to prevent any unintended or unscheduled departures of the residents, the dining and living rooms are cozy and very personal, not at all institutional and sterile. Yet the thing I loved most that I knew would well suit my Mom was the small number of residents, six at most.

On the day I visited, it was lunch time and the residents were sitting at the dining room table. Even though they all couldn't recall each other's names, they were interacting and engaged in friendly small talk. Those expressions of communal fellowship are what I consider the simple pleasures of life. Two of the residents were looking out of the windows commenting to each other on how beautiful a day it was. To observe two ninety-five year olds chatting so amiably was thrilling for me. One of the other residents asked my Mom, "Are you going to move here?" My Mom answered simply, "I don't know. You have to ask my daughter." So I asked my Mom if she liked the group home. She thought for a minute and asked, "Do they have dessert after dinner?" Ms. Mamie chimed in, "We have dessert after every meal". My Mom then asked, "Is there a bathroom here?" We assured her that there was. She then said, "Then I like it!" And so it was done. My Mom was moving to Mamie's Loving Care. She had a choice of bedrooms and she picked the one she liked. I chose a group home for my Mom as opposed to an assisted living facility for dementia patients because I want my Mom to be relaxed and comfortable and she certainly seemed to be so at Mamie's Loving Care.

I hurriedly packed my Mom's belongings at Friendship Terrace. As I was paying Kathy, the home health aide, to watch my Mom night and day, I wanted the transition to occur as quickly as possible. Kathy truly had saved the day for our family. She, in the right place at the right time, also personally benefited greatly. As my Mom moved into a furnished bedroom it meant that she had no further need for the furniture in her studio apartment, all of which Tim and I gave *and* delivered to Kathy's home for use by her sons. I was so grateful that Kathy had taken such good care of my Mom that I gave her a generous tip for her eight days of service.

Eight days! I could not believe I had found a new place for my Mom, packed her belongings, and prepared to move her to her new place in only eight days. I was proud of that. Yet I also felt sad that I had waited so long to move my Mom and, thus, unnecessarily risked her personal safety and security. I know I was lucky that she didn't leave her stove on and set the place on fire, take too many of her thyroid pills in a moment of forgetfulness, or walk outside of her building failing to recall where she lived.

Still, with all this said, I admitted to myself that I hadn't wanted to move my Mom because I didn't want to accept that her condition was worsening.

As my Mom's dementia progressed, serious patience was required.

Chapter V - Patience Is A Virtue

You know the expression, patience is a virtue. Frequently, people remark how patient I am with my Mom. Others have asked me for advice on how they can be more patient with their elderly loved ones. So, what is patience anyway?

According to Merriam-Webster's online dictionary, patience is defined as the capacity to accept or tolerate delay, trouble, or suffering without becoming angry or upset.[3] In my view, through the lens of my experience in observing others *and* in coming to know more about myself, patience is a personal quality, an aspect of human character that expresses itself in the act, the art of being tranquil, at peace in the face of difficulty.

Through my six years thus far of direct engagement with the disease of dementia, which can test the souls of the most tolerant, patience truly has been a virtue. One of the things I have learned is that patience is not simply a mindset. It has to become a lifestyle, a daily way of being.

I've often wondered what it is about dementia that makes sufferers repeat themselves. Whatever type of dementia my Mom has causes her say the same words and to ask the same question over and over and over again. Whenever my Mom sees me, her first question is, "What are we doing today?" I answer. A few seconds later,

---

[3] Patience. (n.d.) In Merriam-Webster Dictionary online. Retrieved from http://www.merriam-webster.com/dictionary/patience

"What are we doing today?" I answer. A few more seconds "What are we doing today?" I answer again. And again. And again. And again.

There have been many occasions when my Mom's repetition of the same question distresses me, perhaps because with each asking I am reminded that she has changed and is changing, thus, no longer the mother I have known. I get through each of those moments one at a time. When I was sick and in a lot of pain, I remember thinking, "I just want this to stop". When my Mom's repetition becomes heartrending, for example, during the occasion of a long car ride, I do think to myself, "I just want this to stop." Every now and then, I believe it is difficult for my Mom, for she'll ask, "Did I already say that?"

When people inquire as to how I can be so patient with my Mom, I think it's a strange question because I don't think I could be impatient with her. People seem to think I "taught myself" to be patient. I wouldn't say that, but I do believe that I've worked hard on being patient because, most simply and profoundly, she is my Mom, the woman who gave birth, life to me.

I also did a little research on the topic. I found a great article, "The Importance of Being Patient" from the website, Code of Living. For me, one of the article's most meaningful observations is that patience "is one of the most important things a person can cultivate and every person should strive to become very patient."[4] I took this to mean that, despite the disposition of one's nature, whether more or less forbearing, being patient can be a

---

[4] Hameed, Osman. The importance of being patient. Code of Living. Retrieved from http://www.codeofliving.com/how-be-more-patient

personal determination, a conscious choice, an act of one's will. I decided that being more patient would work not only in and with my relationship with my Mom, but also with my husband, Tim. Coming to that discernment and having put it into daily practice, definitely has been more than worth the effort.

Concerning putting it into practice, one of the article's points that got my attention was that to become more patient, one has to realize that one's current level of tolerance has its roots in the earliest, most formative years.[5] I thought back to my childhood to assess how patient I was as a kid because, as the article states, most children begin with a very low level of patience unless their parents were firm and made them wait for the things that they wanted, in other words, teaching their children the life's lesson of deferring instant gratification. This was one of my Mom's most faithfully imparted teachings.

When my Mom began to repeat herself, it was obvious to me that I was going to have to really stretch and stand outside of my comfort zone, a point that the article also emphasizes.

The article's five points that have helped me to improve and continue to focus on my level of patience are below. I've also included how these insights have been shaped throughout my life to this point.

A. Understand and Counteract Your Triggers

"Impatience is something that is triggered. This trigger is different for everybody but it has the same purpose. Try

---

[5] (Hameed 2012)

to understand what your trigger is. What is that 'thing' you think about or feel right before you lose it?"[6]

When I read about impatience and triggers, my Mom was the first person who popped into my mind. The triggers I had to overcome had to do with timing. Prior to my Mom being diagnosed with dementia, she was *always* organized and on time. She hated it when others were tardy, considering lateness a mark of rudeness, and taught Renee and me, as an expression of our consideration for others, always to be on time. When her dementia arrived, that philosophy went out the proverbial window. My Mom was always searching for something, whether her ID, keys, or purse which usually made her late. When we had made plans to go somewhere, I'd call her in advance, saying that I was in route, alerting her to make her final preparations to depart, and then, when a few minutes away, I'd call again.

As my Mom's dementia progressed, I eventually took all of her important belongings, her ID, her purse, so that we wouldn't have to spend so much time searching for them. Initially and understandably, she was furious, but then (and this is one of the ironic "blessings" of the disease), she soon forgot that she was angry. She would be thrilled when we arrived at her doctor's office and I had her ID and insurance cards. She'd say, "I was just wondering where I put those."

Before departing on a trip of any length, time also has been spent waiting for my Mom to go to the rest room. Typically, she will tell me repeatedly that she needs to go, having forgotten that she already had gone. Usually, I will

---

[6] (Hameed 2012)

have her go twice, and then say, "We'll be at the place in less than five minutes where there is a restroom." Almost always, she will say, "OK," and we head to the car.

After much thought, I determined that a trigger for me is tardiness or when things do not happen in a timely manner. Thus, I began building 15 or 20 minutes into our schedule so I wouldn't become impatient when the time of my Mom's appointment drew near.

To counteract the trigger of my Mom's repetitive speech, I exercise my patience by pretending each time that she says something that I am hearing it for the first time. This approach has worked incredibly well. My anxiety doesn't rise and neither does my voice. My tone is modulated and I avoid responding with the retorts, "You just asked me that" or "Don't ask me that again!" I confess that every now and then, I still think those things, but I do not allow myself to say them.

B. Build Self-Confidence

I felt the article was speaking directly to me when it explained the genesis or source of the impatience.

"Impatience usually appears when you feel let down, when you don't feel in control, or perhaps feel that your hands are tied. You want something to happen now, but you cannot seem to do anything to speed things up. A person with a high level of confidence will accept the situation as it is and not fight or rail against it, but rather will work with it, realizing that patience and confidence go hand in hand."[7]

---

[7] (Hameed 2012)

Reflecting on the article's insights about the roots of patience going back to childhood and that patience is tied to confidence, it brought back some very interesting memories for me. As a child I did everything quickly. I remember many times my Mom telling me, often in reference to my school work, "Just be patient. Everyone doesn't do things as fast as you do". Although my Mom praised me when I did well in school, I didn't have a great deal of overall confidence in myself. I now know that some of that lack can be attributed to the absence of my father and my utter incomprehension as to why he was not in my life.

As I got older and my confidence increased, so did my patience. Capitalizing on my Mom's lesson on deferred gratification, I knew that I didn't have to have everything right now. I was able to relax and let things happen, especially, once dementia came into our lives, when it came to my Mom. I quickly grasped that neither my Mom nor I had any control over this disease, so we may as well go with the flow.

C. Put On Your "Positive" Glasses

Of all the article's recommendations, this was and is my favorite for increasing patience. The article stated that patience, "is all about perspective and how you look at situations and putting a positive spin on everything".[8] That quote could be my mantra. I always have embraced an incredibly positive attitude, especially regarding my many years of illness given that none of my doctors thought that I would reach the age of forty.

---

[8] (Hameed 2012)

I always try to put an optimistic spin on everything that happens, especially in relation to my time spent with my Mom. One of the ways I deal with her repetition and other uncomfortable aspects of her disease is by telling myself that it could be far worse. Although this may seem a Pollyannaish attitude in the face of real difficulty, I do believe that it could be worse, for example, my Mom not remembering me, who I am or what I do. One of the most positive things about my Mom repeating things is that she does tell me how much she appreciates everything I do for her. I have to admit that I don't mind hearing that over and over again. Another *extremely* positive thing is that as I was growing up my Mom didn't say very often, "I love you." Now, given the increasingly severe limitations of her short term memory, as I leave her after our visits, she says again and again, "Love you." That's priceless for me.

There are many positives about my "new" Mom, the most important of which is the fact that she doesn't remember most of the causes or experiences of her anxiety. When we go out these days, she can ride in the car for hours without saying once, "Is that car coming into our lane?" or "Look out!" or my personal favorite, "You're a great driver. It's everyone else I'm worried about."

D. Change Your Attitude

The article, explaining that most people who desire more patience don't know why they are in such a hurry to get everything done, suggests keeping an open perspective to reduce stress.[9]

---

[9] (Hameed 2012)

I had to change my attitude or approach to life for a different reason. Although I have learned not to rush and I long have cultivated a positive outlook, I did need to change my attitude about hating this disease because there is no need to hate anything or anyone. Once dementia arrives, it is here to stay. All we can do is accept it and do the best we can. I miss my "old" Mom, but my attitude about my "new" Mom is new and improved too.

E. Visualize

I was happy to see this as one of the article's final topics. Visualizing involves imagining, painting a mental portrait, indeed, seeing yourself facing the problem before it happens and setting goals for how you want to react.[10]

What I visualize about my Mom's condition is that we will get through a visit or appointment without anything negative or upsetting happening. I visualize the two of us having a great conversation as we often did in former days. I see myself again as a little girl when my Mom took me to the playground and pushed me in a swing or when we together rode the amusement rides at Hershey Park. Picturing my Mom being happy, I am able to remember the good things in her life. Some of her most contented memories that she still recalls are playing the card game bid whist on Friday nights with her girlfriends, watching the Alvin Ailey dancers perform "Revelations", wearing outfits in fashion shows that she handcrafted with her women's sewing group, taking college classes as an older adult after Renee and I finished our degrees, and mastering all of the Tai Chi moves. She continues to

---

[10] (Hameed 2012)

visualize all these experiences and, in our enjoyment, we laugh about them often.

The article also includes some excellent motivational quotes that I love and list here in the event that they help others.

Motivational Quotes

- A man who is a master of patience is master of everything else. *George Savile*
- Patience is a necessary ingredient of genius. *Benjamin Disraeli*
- It is hard! But what cannot be removed becomes lighter through patience. *Horace*
- He that can have patience can have what he will. *Benjamin Franklin*
- I have just three things to teach: simplicity, patience, compassion. These three are your greatest treasures. *Lao Tzu*
- Patience and perseverance have a magical effect before which difficulties disappear and obstacles vanish. *John Quincy Adams*[11]

One of the challenges of being my Mom's mom, simply put, arises when she doesn't want to do what I need her to do. Although I didn't meet my daughter Kim, Tim's child born to his first marriage, until she was eight years old, I did help raise her during her teenage years. I remember her strong will and resistance to rules. My Mom often reminds me of a resistant child. I moved her to a safe environment and she says, "You took me out of DC. I never wanted to leave there." I dress her in a really nice outfit and she protests "I don't want to wear that!", and

---

[11] (Hameed 2012)

then quickly changes her clothes. I tell her that we have to go to a doctor's appointment and she resists saying, "I don't want to go. I don't like needles".

The title of this book, Being My Mom's Mom, came to me after a verbal tussle with her about going to the doctor. My Mom blurted out, "You're acting like the Mom!" Instantly we broke out in laughter. When I told her I was writing a book about her, she said, "Who would want to read a book about me?" I'm guessing that there will be at least a few people who will read, and, I hope, profit from reading this book.

In addition to needing patience with my Mom, I also must summon a similar degree and depth of tolerance for the many people we encounter who stare at her and comment under their breaths about how often she has repeated herself. I have had encounters with those who have said to me, "I would kill myself if my mother repeated things all the time" and "Do you know how many times she asked you that?" and "How do you stand it?" When people snicker aloud about my Mom, I don't take it personally. I suppose they don't, perhaps can't understand that she's not repeating herself intentionally or purposefully saying peculiar things. And I do feel that I have to protect my Mom when anyone utters an unkind comment to her. I just hold her hand more tightly and we move on.

I began this chapter writing that patience truly is a virtue. I've learned to give my Mom everything she needs, especially my patience because she deserves it. Every day, I work harder to be the most lovingly, gently forbearing daughter I can be. I know that I'll have to learn to be even more tolerant as her disease progresses. What will my

Mom be like in a few years? How will I feel if *and* when she forgets who I am? Will I then still be as patient? I hope the answer to that question will be YES.

This is my greatest fear. That I will not be as patient with my Mom as her personality continues to change and she becomes less and less my "old" Mom and more my "new" Mom. I'm a realist, so I know that the nice sweet person that my Mom is today may not, perhaps likely will not last. I know it's possible that she will become difficult and combative as opposed to the stubborn person she can be today. As hard as this disease has been to this point, I know it could be so much worse. In addition to visualizing the past and the present, I've also visualized the future in an attempt to prepare myself for whatever I may face. As I write this, I'm preparing myself financially, taking on a job to finance my Mom's future care.

I hope you can find an article or some other motivation to find the patience when you need it. It's not always easy, but I believe it's helpful to acknowledge and to accept that no one ever asks or desires to become a dementia sufferer and that none of it, the onset of the disease and the ongoing outcomes, is the fault of your loved one.

Chapter VI - Keep Hope and Humor Alive

Every day is different, so be ready for anything. Two things that I've found have really helped me with this disease are hope and humor.

Hope is defined in Merriam-Webster's dictionary as "expectation of obtainment, confident anticipation of what is to come".[12] It may not make much sense to hope for anything positive when it comes to dementia, but there is always at least one optimistic thing that helps you move through the day.

I share my top five "Loretta-isms", self-encouragements, which I hope may be helpful for you in dealing with dementia. They definitely give me hope!

> 1) *Focus on the memories* – Every family has fond memories. Once dementia enters the family, it's great to look back, reflect on and relish in the events that happened in the years gone by. For my Mom, it's what she remembers, which, in many ways is all she has. I love engaging her in conversation about the things that still matter and make sense to her. I've learned some things that I didn't know about her first jobs. It was at one of those early employments that my Mom met Mrs. Adams. Their favorite saying is that they "met

---

[12] Hope. (n.d.) Merriam-Webster Online Dictionary. http://www.merriam-webster.com/dictionary/hope

over the scrub buckets." My Mom also has shared wonderful reminiscences about her high school years. I've also come to realize that the memories we are making today are and will be only for me because my Mom isn't going to remember them. Acknowledging this reality is helpful, allowing me to relinquish my desire that we do all the things we did in the past, for she will have no lasting, even often current memory of them.

2) *Today may be better than yesterday* – There are times when I want to curse dementia for invading my family. When those moments arise, I tell myself that the next visit with my Mom will be better than the last. That has helped me tremendously. Before I adopted this outlook, I would be very anxious before I visited my Mom. What state of mind would she be in today? Will she be able to enjoy the day? Will I get her back before the late afternoon "sundown effect" appears, manifesting itself in my Mom's intensified anxiety? Now, reciting my phrase to myself before I see my Mom, I can lower my degree of worry, and over time, I have found our visits to be fruitful regardless of her state of mind and being.

3) *This day is almost over* – The last part of any visit with my Mom is usually the most challenging for me. I try to schedule only one activity per outing. Like most people, I think, when I'm doing errands, I try to do several in the same trip. A couple of years ago, I realized that doesn't work with my Mom. When we are going to the doctor, we can do only that and maybe lunch, but not

doctor, lunch, and then visit relatives. By the time we got to the third event or errand, my Mom was worn out and no longer enjoying herself and, frankly, not that much fun to be around. I've never figured out if getting in and out of the car several times is what causes a spike in my Mom's anxiety, but, I think, that's possible. When we go to lunch and sit there for several hours working on Seek and Find Word puzzles, she is perfectly fine. Yet when we go to three places, even if it takes barely an hour, she's restless, agitated, and wants to go home. Sitting in a McDonald's for hours is one of my Mom's favorite things to do. As an adult, you would never have caught my Mom in a McDonald's, however, today, she seems to find some comfort in the place. I used to take her to Starbuck's, but it didn't appear to be nearly as calming or cheering a locale for her. The lesson for me is we need to find a place that "works" for our loved ones and keep going there until it no longer proves beneficial.

4) *It was a great night* – There have been times when my Mom was fine throughout the course of an evening activity. BUT I've learned that I have to coordinate with the primary care giver to administer her anti-anxiety medications, usually given at night, earlier in the afternoon. At the end of one of our rare evening events, I am so thankful that no catastrophe has occurred. It's funny to me how something so relatively small as attending a concert or a play is fulfilling to me. Yet, when accompanied by my Mom and without difficulty or mishap, my experience is heightened with deep

gratitude. Having written this, this disease has taught me that it, my life in relationship with my Mom, is not about me, and that my wants and needs are always secondary to hers. I remember my Mom always putting Renee and me first when we were kids. Now I do the same for her.

5) *Take a photo because you can't get this moment back* – I probably drive people crazy (at least that's what they tell me!) with all of the photos I take. This is one area where I imitate my Mom. She always was taking pictures of us as children and later, as adults with our own families. I don't remember where I first saw this, but one recommendation for coping with dementia is to make a visual record of everything done and seen with the patient. Thankfully, my Mom doesn't mind taking photos or being photographed, perhaps because she doesn't remember that it's happened. As a practical benefit, having snapshots in hand has helped me provide answers for my Mom, especially when she is argumentative. Trying to convince her that we've been to a certain place, that we've just eaten, or that we've already seen what she is asking to see proved nearly impossible before I started taking photos of everything. When my Mom says fussily, "I don't know why you won't let me get dessert", I quickly show her the picture of her enjoying her cake, pie, or ice cream barely minutes earlier. Once she sees the "evidence" realizing that she has on the exact outfit that she's wearing and is sitting in exactly the same place her protests immediately end. I also take the

photos for myself. Seeing the smile on my Mom's face as we spend time with her sister Frannie or the wonder on her face as we enjoy a Cirque du Soleil production truly are priceless. In many ways her childlike wonder and amazement are things that give me hope in my sense of the promise that she is feeling the same joy that her expressions project.

I've always researched alternative and non-traditional therapies and want to mention two here as possible vehicles for hope.

Music Therapy

I loved an article I found on the A Place for Mom website at www.aplaceformom.com about a certified music therapist, Concetta Tomaino, who is the director of the Institute for Music and Neurologic Function at Beth Abraham Family of Health Services in New York.[13] Ms. Tomaino has had amazing success with dementia patients using music. In one case, she worked with a man who had not spoken for several years. She began singing to him and within a month he was trying to speak and eventually began to sing the song. He continued to recover his capacity to speak, living many years thereafter. I was fascinated and excited by Ms. Tomaino's research about music and brain function. She writes:

> Music that has personal significance to someone or is connected with historical events is a strong stimulus to engage responses in people, even in

---

[13] Dementia Therapy and Music. (n.d,) A Place for Mom.
http://alzheimers.aplaceformom.com/articles/dementia-therapy-and-music

late stages of dementia. Even if they're not necessarily able to tell you what the song is, they are able to be moved and feel the associations.

Ms. Tomaino explained that we process, that is, perceive and interpret music with almost every part of our brain. As such, and that in both early and late stages of dementia, music can "retune the brain, (improving) memory (lowering) agitation, and (improving) cognitive skills". In later stages of dementia, music can be of help in "maintaining motor skills, reducing anxiety and increasing attention and focus."[14]

One of the things I really loved about Ms. Tomaino's work is that she uses instruments such as drums, harps, and the human voice to engage her patients. In one case, a wife played an autoharp for her husband, and, in response, he quite apart from his customary behavior of staring straight ahead in silence and stillness, began to move his legs in time with the rhythm.

A most encouraging aspect about music therapy as I perceive it is that it provides hope when we get a glimpse, however momentary, of the loved one we used to know as they "come back" for an instant or two to sing or dance like they did in former days. As the disease takes so much from our loved ones, if music can give them back to us, even for a few minutes, that for me, is a cause of rejoicing! My Mom's own experience with music has been interesting. I have noticed that there are songs of which she still remembers the melodies and the lyrics, especially those of that great songstress Whitney Houston.

---

[14] A Place for Mom http://alzheimers.aplaceformom.com/articles/dementia-therapy-and-music

When my Mom and I watched movies when I was younger, it was usually a musical. Our favorite is The Sound of Music. We must have watched it dozens of times. I know the words to every song. In 2011, Tim and I went to Austria and Switzerland and, of course, we took the Sound of Music tour. Throughout the excursion, I thought of my Mom. When I moved her into the group home in 2009, to ensure she could watch the musicals she so loved, I purchased a DVD player and several discs of my Mom's favorites, including The Sound of Music, The King and I, Seven Brides for Seven Brothers, and West Side Story.

In my efforts to work with my Mom to keep her mind stimulated, I have been assisted by the nurse who visits the group home monthly. Some time ago, she called me to tell me that she had found an Episcopal Church hymnal and was using it with my Mom. As my Mom and I are both cradle Episcopalians, we know a goodly number of the hymns by heart. The nurse told me that she would sing a verse and my Mom would sing the next verse. I was delightfully shocked, for I never had heard my Mom sing without the hymnal in front of her.

Pet Therapy

Pet therapy is another alternative that offers many benefits, bolstering hope for dementia patients and their families. According to Mara Baun, a coordinator of the PhD in nursing program at the University of Texas Health Sciences Center at the Houston School of Nursing, people with dementia can recognize a dog or cat on sight and, usually, will want to interact with the animal.[15]

Ms. Baun's amazing study compared how adults in Alzheimer's units related socially with and without the presence of an animal, especially a dog. She found the prevalence of heightened interaction whenever the pet was present. In addition to stimulating social response, the research indicated a variety of benefits for dementia patients.

- A lessening frequency and intensity in agitation behaviors.
- An increase in physical activity, especially when the patient is able to groom or engage in play with the animal.
- An improvement of appetite.
- A heightening of enjoyment in companionship.[16]

My Mom never was a fan of pets. (When I was growing up, she allowed me to have a turtle!) However, I have seen the benefit derived by other people with dementia through their engagement with animals. When my sister Renee was in a nursing home, the residents always perked up excitedly when the pets came to visit, especially my niece Nia's dog "Izzy" who loved all the attention.

Whatever you can do for your loved one, please, repeating, as a word of encouragement, the title of Chapter IV, just do it! It helps and it gives us all hope. So

---

[15] Vann, Madeline. How animal therapy helps dementia patients. Everyday Health. Retrieved from at http://www.everydayhealth.com/alzheimers/how-animal-therapy-helps-dementia-patients.aspx

[16] (Vann 2012)

sing, dance, clap, borrow your neighbor's dog for two days a month. Do anything and everything to bring a smile to your loved one and to the entire family. Seeing my Mom smile is, as the commercial would say, *priceless*!

Humor

There is nothing funny about dementia. However, there are moments when situations, generated by the disease can be hysterical. My Mom is so funny I've thought about selling a book of her quotes or getting her a show as a stand-up comedian. Humor is mandatory for coping with this disease.

Not surprisingly, much research has been done on the benefits of using humor with dementia patients. A study by Dr. Lee-Fay Low found that humor worked better than antipsychotic drugs to manage agitation. Dr. Low examined how humor affected moods and agitation in patients in 36 residential care facilities in Australia. Staff members were taught a humor therapy program called "Play Up".

The patients in the study experienced a "20 percent reduction in agitated behaviors such as physical and verbal aggression, wandering, screaming, and repetitive behaviors and questions."[17] The program lasted twelve weeks and the beneficial results continued through that time and for the twenty-six week follow up. (Unfortunately, with the conclusion of the visits of the humor practitioner, the positive results came to an end.)

---

[17] Nauert, PhD, R. (2011) Humor Therapy Helps Manage Dementia. Psych Central. Retrieved on September 4, 2012 from http://psychcentral.com/news/2011/09/22/humor-therapy-helps-manage-dementia/29692.html

One writer who used her blog to share the challenges of caring for her mother, started a goal in her home of "A Laugh a Day". I love this idea! There have been several occasions when I have sent friends and family members funny things that my Mom has said, calling my text or email "your laugh of the day." Several of the recipients have told me, "This makes my day!" It makes me feel better, too.

I know my Mom has given her caregivers numerous occasions to laugh. At present, my Mom has been in her group home for three years, her room located down the hall a few feet from the front door. Yet each and every time she returns from a trip to the rest room in the home or from an outing with me, the first thing she says is "Where do I go?" We all chuckle about that. Still at the same time, it's scary to think of what would happen if my Mom ever wandered outside alone.

The caregivers also giggle when my Mom wets a washcloth, washes her face, and considers herself having taken a shower. Much like a child, they, reminding her that she's not done, run the water for her so that she can complete her bathing. It's funny watching my Mom try to get away with something, for example, to avoid taking her shower, rushing back to her room to read a book she's read countless times.

In completing my research for this chapter, I can use my findings to reflect on and relish in all the hope and humor that are still present in my Mom and in her situation. I'll continue to work as hard as I can to make her feel special and loved and to comfort her when she's having a bad moment. I have hope for the future that whatever comes, I'll be ready. While none of us can know what tomorrow may bring, we, relying on the strength of optimism and the solace of laughter, can carry on and through.

Chapter VII - Heartbreak

Heartbreak strikes everyone where dementia is concerned, those suffering from the disease and those caring for them. There will be times when you will break your loved one's heart attempting to do what's best. Just accept the fact that this will happen and try to prepare yourself for it as much as you can.

I've also learned that this disease requires letting go of a lot of things: anger at your loved one for past deeds done that ought not to have been done, anguish about family secrets buried in the memories of your loved one that never will be explained to your satisfaction, discontent about loans that never may be repaid and, hence, have to be considered as gifts, and distress concerning unresolved disagreements. Still, with so much that we need to relinquish, there always is one thing that we are obliged to keep in hand: the need to share our compassion in the provision of care for our loved one.

(When I read about parent or elder abuse, I always wonder about the causes. I know there are parents who have been and are abusive in their relations with their children. However, I still find it difficult to imagine what could drive adult children to abuse their loved ones, short of having been victims of molestation or other emotional, physical or psychological deprivations. Even in such cases, before resorting to elder abuse, I believe that professional assistance or intervention is to be sought to ensure that the loved one and family members receive the necessary therapy, treatment, or even legal remediation.)

The hardest thing about this disease is the sense of helplessness. When life is difficult, we want to make things better. Dementia, however, allows no easy course toward the improvement or enhancement of life. Dementia is something you simply can't "fix".

In becoming my Mom's mom, I've already experienced several heartbreaking moments. I've grown from each of them and have tried to learn from the impossible to avoid mistakes I've made along the way.

First, there was the day that I had to take my Mom's checkbook, explaining to her that from that point on, I was going to write all the checks. Understandably, she didn't take it well, asking, "Why can't I keep my checkbook, and then you come over here and watch me while I write the checks?" I tried to explain to her that it was for her own good. Hearing myself say that I realized then that I was my Mom's parent. I couldn't begin to count how many times during my childhood that she said to me, "I'm doing this for your own good." I hated hearing that and swore that if I ever had children, I would *never* say that to them. And now, I heard myself say it to my Mom. That was a real "aha" moment for me. I was so afraid that she would be the victim of some sort of fraud, for it was easy to talk her into writing a check for any reason. Moreover, as she had never used an ATM card, when I took her checkbook from her, she felt helpless and betrayed. On that day, leaving her, as I walked out the door, she yelled, "I don't have any money now! Give me my money back!" She was angry with me for quite a while. Months later, we were riding down the highway and out of the blue she said, "I'm glad you're paying all the bills now because now I can focus on the fun stuff." Feeling incredibly relieved, I smiled and said, "That's right!"

The first weekend in June of 2008 was a life changing moment. My dear friend Pontheolla arranged a fabulous celebration for her husband Paul. It was entitled "30-20-10" in recognition of his 30 years of ministry as an Episcopal priest, the 20 years he had served in the Episcopal Diocese of Washington, and the 10 years he had been Rector of St. Mark's Episcopal Church, Capitol Hill. I had promised Pontheolla that I'd arrive early on Friday night to help setup and prepare for the first event. Prior to going to church, I visited my Aunt Frannie. We had a nice visit and as I got ready to leave, Frannie asked me to sit down because she wanted to tell me something. She shared that she wanted me to know that she and my father were friends and that he loved me very much. I had no idea that they were acquainted with each other in any real way. Her revelation came as a thrilling surprise. Then she dropped a bombshell. My father desperately had desired to be a vital part in my life, but that my Mom had prevented it. Once it was revealed that my father was gay, my Mom told him that he never again would be allowed to see Renee and me. For minutes, I sat there speechless, trying to grasp this new and jarring information. My first impulse was to get up and run. At the same time, I recognized in my aunt's disclosure something that sounded like a truth from which I could not, dare not run, for, in that instant, so much about which I had been confused was made clear. And as we all know, you can't run from the truth.

All of my life, I had believed that my father had left us, never attempting to see us again because that's how he wanted it. To discover forty-nine years later that my Mom was the reason I never had an opportunity to have a relationship with my father was heartbreaking. For several moments following Frannie's confession, I found it hard to breathe. After a while, still stunned, I got up. I had committed myself to help Pontheolla. I left Frannie and drove to our church, but I have little memory of that trip, my arrival, and my lending aid. I was totally absorbed, mind, heart, and soul on what I had learned about my parents.

Now that I had this information, what was I supposed to do with it? As upset as I was with my Mom about this family secret, I also knew that my Mom and I never would be able to have a conversation about it. This was information with which I could do absolutely nothing, *except* finally to revel in the knowledge that my father, my Dad loved me! After that night's event at church, I shared my Aunt Frannie's revelation with Paul and Pontheolla. Paul was incredulous and asked, "You heard this information for the first time and you still came here tonight?" "Yes", I replied, "I never considered not coming." It was such a disturbing discovery that I suppose I felt I would be able to cope more easily with the torrent of emotions that were roiling within me if I were around lots of people.

That very night, I forgave my Mom for keeping my Dad from me and moved on. Did I want to do that? No, I longed to ask her why she did that, and why, after Renee and I became adults, she did not let us decide whether we wanted to have a relationship with our Dad. However, as my Mom's caregiver and chief source of financial support, what real choice did I have? If I punished her now for something she did almost fifty years ago, she wouldn't understand what was happening, so what would be the point? My Mom understands so little about the complex, even commonplace occurrences of daily living that I'd never consider further complicating her life by venting my anger, treating her badly, or withholding my love.

The next day, I had an epiphany. I learned that you could grieve for someone who hadn't died. This deeply felt, clearly perceived awareness came to light in a most unusual way. During the events of the weekend, I met many members of Paul and Pontheolla's families, including Pontheolla's mother, Geneva Watkins, to whom I found myself powerfully drawn. If Geneva was sitting, I sat next to her. If she was talking, I listened. If she asked me a question, I answered in great detail. After a while, I realized how much of her time I had monopolized. What I didn't understand right away was why. Then I heard myself telling her how much I missed having conversations with my Mom and how thankful I was to her for allowing me to attach myself to her. Then it hit me. Although my Mom was physically alive, in Geneva, I was seeking a mother. The next day, I called Pontheolla and apologized for dominating her mother's time, and explained that I had realized that I was grieving for my Mom. Thankfully, Pontheolla comforted me, telling me that no apology was necessary and that she happily would share her mother with me. That was a moment I will never forget.

I experienced another heartbreak when I packed my Mom's belongings for her move to the group home. I discovered that some of our oldest family photos, many that my grandparents entrusted to my Mom, were missing. Given my Mom's behavior of throwing things away, I was upset with myself that I had not protected better these irreplaceable family treasures. Now, they were gone, and I was heartsick. After a while, I stopped beating myself up, for I realized that no one was left to blame me but me. Again, I moved on.

Still another heartbreak occurred the day I moved my Mom out of Washington, DC, the only place she had lived for her eighty years. As we headed toward the door of her old apartment carrying the last box of her belongings, she started to cry. I gave her a big hug and asked if she was OK. She held on to me tightly and pleaded, "I'll be good. Please don't make me move". As gently as I could, I told her that she hadn't been "bad" and that I was moving her for her own safety. She didn't understand that it had become dangerous for her to live alone. She viewed the move as punishment for something she had done wrong. Walking over that threshold and taking my Mom to Maryland was the hardest thing I've ever had to do, especially as my decision reduced my Mom to tears. I had to force myself to keep walking and not give in to her pleas and tears. I never thought it would be so hard. "Where am I going to live now?", she asked as we got on the elevator for the last time. I explained that I lived in Clinton, Maryland, and that now she was going to live in Maryland too just ten minutes from me. We took photos of a few of her friends and walked hand in hand to the car. My Mom kept her head down all the way and never looked back at the retirement community that had been her home for 10 years.

Dropping my Mom off at Mamie's Loving Care was excruciatingly painful. On the day I signed the lease, Ms. Mamie suggested that I come with all of my Mom's belongings, and then leave her alone with them. Huh? I couldn't help her get her settled? On second thought, I did understand why Ms. Mamie had implemented that rule. If the caregivers and my Mom together put her belongings away in the room, they all would know where everything was, and, more importantly, begin to form a bond of relationship. Even so, I felt like I was abandoning my Mom in much the same way, I think, as some parents feel as they drop their kids off at day care or kindergarten. My heart was breaking. Why was it so hard? I didn't expect to experience such an overwhelming flood of emotion. I barely made it to my car before the tears came, pouring from my eyes and coursing down my cheeks. My tears were those of sadness for my Mom in yet another stage in the reduction of her independence. My tears also were signs of my guilt that I wasn't bringing my Mom home to live with me. Yet, in spite of my remorse, I knew that forcing my Mom to live with Tim and me would have served no good purpose. She had always told Renee and me that she *never* wanted to meddle in our lives and especially that she never wanted to live with either one of us. We had heard that more than a thousand times. Our response was always the same, "Yes, Mom we know." In 1998, when we moved my Mom to the retirement community, she made us promise that if she ever lost her capacity to think for herself that we would not bring her to live with us, ending her plea with the dramatic and unforgettable declaration, "I would just die." My Mom, for whatever her reasons believed that having to live with your children somehow equaled the irrevocable loss of personal dignity. Renee and I surmised that my Mom's sense of things had something to do with the fact that she lived with her parents for her entire adult life. So we vowed to her that we would comply with her wishes. Over the years, as I took on more responsibility for her care, I was determined not to go back on my word. To do so would be to betray my Mom's most heartfelt and professed desire. In moving her to the group home, I kept my promise to her in maintaining her dignity, which clearly was more important to her than I had realized.

My Mom had been so active in her retirement community that my biggest fear was that she'd just wither away at the group home as there were no formal activities, other than meals (which, however, seemed to be my Mom's chief and daily preoccupation). I was determined to keep her active through formal outings, activities, car rides, and walks in the park. However, these engagements were the source not only of heartbreak, but significant financial expense.

Since my teenage years, our family had a wonderful annual tradition. All of us, my Mom, my Aunt Diane, Renee, her daughter Nia (when she was old enough), and I would go to the Kennedy Center in Washington, DC, to see the performances of the Dance Theater of Harlem and the Alvin Ailey Dancers. When Tim and I married, our daughter Kim became part of the group. My Mom simply relished the incredible dancers, their artistic prowess and creativity, always wanting more, growing sad as the show drew to its close. The first year my Mom moved to the group home, the excursion to the Kennedy Center was uneventful and, as usual, she loved it. The next year, as we sat through the Alvin Ailey production, she didn't seem to be quite "with it." She clapped after each dance presentation, but appeared distracted. I didn't worry at first as her favorite dance, "Revelations", had not yet been performed. When that dance began, she stared straight ahead without any seeming recognition. As I always want my Mom to find her enjoyment in life, I was disappointed, but tried not to show it. I quietly said to her, "This is your favorite dance." She replied with an unenthused, "Uh huh."

When the performance ended, we headed to the restroom. My Mom was carrying her program as we stood in line. "Did you have a good time?", I asked. She answered "What did we do?" For an instant I was perplexed, finally saying, "The performance of the Alvin Ailey Dancers." She looked at me, peering into my eyes as if searching for meaning, and then said, "Oh, we used to come see them a lot". She hadn't understood (even though I had spent quite a bit of money for front row seats). In the noise of the departing crowd, I decided that would not be a fruitful time to pursue it, so I said nothing more. As the rest room line moved along slowly, my Mom looked down at the program in her hand and blurted out loudly, "I love the Alvin Ailey dancers! Why don't you take me to see them anymore?" Several women turned around to look at my Mom. I calmly replied, "I know you love them, *and* we just saw them a few minutes ago". My Mom said, "You must have taken someone else and just gave me the program. I'm not stupid! I'd remember seeing my favorite dance group!" She then turned and walked quickly from the rest room. Usually that would not have posed a problem, but on this day, my right leg was in a walking cast due to a broken ankle. My Mom got a huge head start on me and ran out into the great hallway of the Kennedy Center. I yelled, "Mom, wait!", but she kept walking. Several people looked around and a woman, who recognized what was happening, gently grabbed my Mom by the arm. I caught up with them and thanked the woman. It was the first time my Mom had ever run away from me. I said to her, "I'm sorry you're upset, but trust me we did just see the Alvin Ailey dancers." "Oh, OK, I believe you," she responded, and then with a tremble in her voice, she asked, "But why don't I remember it when it's one of my favorite things to do?" I took her by the hand and into an unoccupied corner away from the crowd. I gave her a big hug. Then we sat down in some nearby chairs, and I went through the program with her. Seeing that the date and time of the performance was that very same day and time, she was convinced that she had been present for the performance. We walked back to the rest room in silence. After a few minutes, she said, "I'm sorry I don't remember. Thank you for bringing me". For whatever reason, perhaps because I interpreted her comment as signifying that, at least for the moment, we had shared an in-the-moment conscious breakthrough, I felt so much better.

While we stood in the still very long rest room line, I pointed out to her all the names of the dances, trying my best to describe the routines and how they unfolded. I wasn't aware that anyone was listening. As I got ready to describe the third dance, a woman behind us chiming in, "Wait, don't forget the other part", began to describe two scenes in the second dance that I had forgotten. I was grateful that what I had sought to give to my Mom, also made sense, perhaps even mattered, to someone else. I said to the woman behind me, "Thank you so much". We embraced, both of us with tears in our eyes. The woman then said, "Keep doing what you're doing. You're doing a great job." I can't describe adequately the feelings that were evoked in me through this episode. I felt beyond helpless. It was just as upsetting for my Mom, for she was beyond exasperated with herself. On the ride home, she repeatedly said, "It costs so much money and I don't even remember it." In that moment, I decided that in the future, we'd only do free fun things so neither one of us would worry or feel regret about the amount of money spent on an event that was instantly forgotten. Although my Mom remembers our family outings of years long gone by to see both Alvin Ailey and the Dance Theater of Harlem, she's never asked about seeing them again.

There was another expensive lesson I learned, sadly, also terribly upsetting for my Mom. I was still a little worried that she wasn't getting enough activity on a daily basis at Ms. Mamie's. Her neurologist had suggested that some of her patients do very well in organized day care where they are exposed to a variety of activities and interactions. So, like any "parent" who wants the best for her "child", I looked into the Crescent Ridge Adult Center about five minutes from the group home. My Mom's roommate at the time went to Crescent Ridge four days a week and wanted my Mom to go too. I took my Mom on a tour of the center, offering a vast array of opportunities for stimulating engagement – bingo, exercise, story time, art and music and field trips. Meals and snacks were also included. My Mom really enjoyed the tour. The center director asked her if she would like to attend the center and she said, "OK, that would be nice". Two days a week was the minimum requirement for participation at a cost of $700 per month. I registered my Mom on the spot. At 8 a.m., a bus picked up my Mom, transporting her to the center and returning her to the group home at 4:30 p.m. On each day of her participation, I would ask, "How was day care? What did you do today?" As she couldn't recall, she'd say simply, "It was fine". I thought she really enjoyed it and that I was doing a great thing to keep my

Mom engaged with the world. Then, I got a call from Angelina, the group home's primary caregiver, who told me, "Your Mom doesn't want to go to day care." Huh? I was very surprised. As I was to learn, my Mom *didn't* like all of the activities they "forced" her to do. She wanted to sit in a corner and read her book as she always did at Ms. Mamie's. She didn't want to have to do something "every minute", she said. Additionally, I discovered that just as my Mom was accustomed to helping out at her old retirement community and at Ms. Mamie's, she preferred, indeed, enjoyed helping the workers set up the snacks and make sandwiches for lunch.

Now, the Crescent Ridge staff hadn't told me of my Mom's displeasure. However, my interaction with the center staff was much more serious than discussing a neglect to inform me that all was not working out as well as I had thought.

One of my Mom's medications prescribed by the neurologist was the anti-anxiety drug called Risperdal, which kept her calm at night. She also took Toporal, a drug designed to slow down her rapid heartbeat. These two medicines combined to induce unconsciousness. My Mom began to suffer from fainting spells. In an instant, she'd say, "I don't feel well", and, in the next moment, she would fall to the floor. One day, a highly unnerved Crescent Ridge staff person called me to tell me my Mom had collapsed and didn't appear to be breathing. This news sent me immediately into a panic. I could hear the voices in the background shouting instructions. I heard someone ask for the AED (automated external defibrillator). Not good, I feared.

I met the ambulance at the hospital and settled my Mom through and out of emergency care, resolving the immediate situation. Subsequently, I met with the center director, sharing a copy of my Mom's hospital reports. At that time, I asked how my Mom was faring in the center program. I was then informed that my Mom liked to be by herself and, thus, it was a challenge to have her participate in the activities. I then thought that perhaps I should consider removing her from the program.

The confirmation of my intuition came the very next week. Angelina called from the group home to say that my Mom had refused to get dressed, saying, "I don't want to go to day care!" I laughed nervously and told Angelina that she could allow my Mom to stay at home that day and that I'd chat with her and the center staff. When I spoke with my Mom about day care, she couldn't describe any of the daily activities. She *did* say, with more than a hint of discontent, "They always want me to do something!" I asked, "What do *you* want to *do* during the day?" "To read my books", she said, "and keep my memory active". (That last comment pleased me greatly.) I then said, "There's no sense paying all that money if you don't want to go". She yelled, "It's not free?" "No, it's not," I said, although daring not to tell her the cost.

I contacted the center giving notice of my intent to take my Mom out of the program. The staff seemed relieved, primarily, I suppose, in addition to the difficulty encountered in encouraging my Mom to join in the daily activities because the cause or causes or my Mom's fainting spells had not yet been determined and surely now there was a precedent for a likely reoccurrence. Thankfully, my Mom doesn't remember that short-lived experiment nor does she recognize the Crescent Ridge center when we drive by. From the moment she was restored to her daily life in the group home, my Mom returned to her bed, stretching out comfortably and reading her books. Happy *and* alone.

To have surgery, at any time in one's life when needed, even urgent, is a serious circumstance. However, to undergo any procedure, particularly when the patient is a dementia sufferer, for a host of other reasons, is a difficult matter. In February of 2011, my Mom had an operation. When she began to have fainting spells, she never could describe what she felt before their occurrences, for she had no memory of the event. The initial tests didn't reveal a cause for the precipitous lowering of her blood pressure, which was the primary presenting cause of her physical distress. A small recording device was to be implanted in her chest to gather detailed information on the moment-by-moment fluctuations in her physical state. The night before her surgery proved to be yet another heartbreaking moment.

My Mom and I had to be at the hospital at 6:00 a.m. I didn't want to disturb the other residents at the group home, so I decided to have my Mom spend the night with Tim and me. In principle, this was a great idea, I thought. However, in practice, it fell woefully short. Of the knowledge and understanding I have amassed about dementia, one essential learning is the necessity of maintaining your loved one's established routine. Once settled, it is best for your loved one and for all to have everything remain the same.

My Mom enjoyed having dinner. Immediately following, she asked, once, twice, and then repeatedly, "OK, when am I going home?" "You're spending the night with us," I said. "Remember?" She protested, "I *have* to go to the other place I live." I assured her that "the other place" knew that she was with us and that everything was alright.

For our post-dinner, pre-bedtime entertainment, we had planned to watch a musical. I had not realized that the group home norm was to watch movies during the day as most of the residents have more difficulty with attention span during the evening hours. For the first fifteen minutes, my Mom watched the television screen, and then she began to pace back and forth across the floor, several times, going to the bathroom, and asking, more urgently as time passed, "When are we going to my other place." I pressed the "stop" button, putting an end to the screening of the movie no one was watching. For the next half hour, Tim and I pleaded with my Mom to put on her pajamas. Throughout, she continued to protest, wanting to go to her "other place," the place she knew, her *real* home. Nothing worked that night to calm her. Not our pleadings. Not her nightly dosage of Respirdal. *Nothing.* "I need to go! I don't want to stay here! They're waiting for me at the other place!" Around midnight, I had half a mind to throw on my coat and take her to the group home, but the timing of the morning's surgery made that impractical. That was the longest night of my life. Somehow (for, to this day, I cannot recall precisely how we managed!), we all, despite having slept less than an hour, survived the night and, the next morning, arrived at the hospital on time, at which point my Mom promptly fell into a deep sleep, lasting through the procedure.

Following the surgery, on the way to her "other place", my Mom, looking at the large bandage on her chest, asked countless times "What's this?" Despite my fatigue, for I had yet to sleep during the procedure, following a restless night, remaining awake and vigilant, consistently, patiently I answered her, recounting the details of the *what* and the *why* of her surgery.

The heartbreak that never goes away for me is stirred whenever I witness the confusion that overwhelms my Mom as afternoon turns to evening. I've learned that I need to coordinate and carry out our activities to the minute, doing all things possible to avoid the ever-present potential for a disaster.

I took my Mom and Mrs. Adams to the Duke Ellington School for the Arts in DC. We saw the musical production, Dreamgirls. The show started at 230 p.m. First, as I was mindful of not keeping my Mom out anywhere near the dinner hour, we had lunch. The show was excellent. We couldn't believe the deeply developed degree of talent of these high school kids. We had a great time, my Mom singing along with the actors.

When the show ended, we went to the rest room. My Mom, holding my hand tightly, seemed terribly uneasy. I thought she might have been uncomfortable by the large crowd of people. Suddenly, loudly, she said, "I don't know what I'm doing!" She looked terrified. I was at a loss. I didn't know what to do or say. I took my Mom to the closest stairwell and sat down with her. Desperately, I scoured my mind, searching for a comforting word. Remembering that we were in Georgetown, a place my Mom spent much of her childhood, quickly I said, "Well, what we did today was to come to Duke Ellington High School to see Dreamgirls and we're now in Georgetown." I could see in her eyes a flickering light of recognition. She said, "OK, let's go outside in Georgetown".

We got through that episode fairly easily and well. Still, I learned yet another lesson that day. Whenever I invite someone to accompany my Mom and me on an outing, that person needs to ride with me to take my Mom home first.

Our ride to take Mrs. Adams home started off beautifully. As they always do, they talked about old times. Then my Mom, increasingly distracted, repeatedly looked at the Dreamgirls program, asking, "What's that?" I answered each time. After we dropped Mrs. Adams off, I realized that it was now almost 5:00 p.m. I still thought all would be well as the ride to the group home should have taken approximately 35 minutes. Alas, as fate would have it, we encountered an accident, and then road construction and the trip quickly took a heartbreaking turn.

The Dreamgirls program became a source of severe agitation for my Mom. She kept saying, "What's this? It isn't mine! Someone left this in your car!" The more she said it, the more aggravated she became. I felt as if she wanted me to stop the car and find out to whom the program belonged or she wouldn't be happy. I suggested that she read through the program, but that brought her no satisfaction. After about 20 minutes of misery, I had an epiphany! Take the program from her and throw it in the back seat! That did the trick! If only I had thought of it 30 minutes earlier!

Due to traffic congestion, it took more than an hour to get back to Ms. Mamie's. During that time, my Mom asked a few hundred times, or so it seemed, "Where are we going?" and "What did we do today?" I wanted to cry, but I continued to answer her questions.

Dementia is at the root of repetition, not only in speech, but also in action. The latter, I hadn't actually seen in my Mom until Christmas 2011 when Tim and I took her to church. My friend Pat had told me about some great puzzles on the Alzheimer's Association website. I loved them and ordered several for my Mom. We wrapped them and had them in the car as we headed to church. We let my Mom open them on the way. She took her time being careful to not tear the paper. She looked and said, "Oooooohhhhh, a puzzle. This, is great! Thank you!" Then she rewrapped them. In the next minute, she looked at the wrapping, asking, "Is it Christmas? Are these mine?" "Yes," we answered as we watched her open her gifts again, accompanied by her more heightened expressions of surprise and greater words of thanks. Within yet another instant, the pattern was repeated. I retrieved the gifts, planning to return them to her following the church service. When we took her home and gave the presents to her, she exclaimed, "Those aren't mine! It's Christmas so you have to give the people their presents". I sighed with a combination of sadness and exasperation. I felt as if I was watching someone in the grips of Obsessive Compulsive Disorder.

Chapter VIII - Take Great Care

This short chapter was added because the phrase "Take great care," is a word of counsel concerning self-care or the care of self that my friend Paul frequently says to me. Given my own medical and physical challenges and the health histories of some of my family members and friends, I care a great deal about and for others. What I have learned and need to remember, which is a lesson that I believe applies to all of us, is that caring for others involves initially caring for ourselves.

I added this chapter after my friend Linda was swamped with taking care of her husband, their five kids, and several friends, all who were facing serious health issues. She was not feeling her best and I said to her, "Please take great care of yourself", that is, *before* you try to take care of others.

The first piece of advice I offer is that you must understand what you can and cannot accomplish. Do not attempt to do everything yourself.

When my Mom lived in the retirement community, I needed a solution for her grocery shopping. It may not seem like much, but at the time I lived 45 minutes from my Mom. Shopping, traveling to my Mom's residence, unpacking and storing the groceries, and returning to my home was a four hour excursion (which was even longer on the trips when I took my Mom with me).

Safeway is my Mom's favorite grocery store. A year before I needed help, the store launched a website Safeway.com, allowing shoppers to select their items online, fill virtual carts, and have their purchases delivered, *and* at the time of the shopper's choosing (it doesn't get any better than that!). It was the perfect situation for my Mom. In paying online, she needed to do nothing except to put the food away once it was delivered. (And there were several people who were willing to store her groceries for her.) I can't account for the amount of time that service saved me, except to say that it was a lot! And my Mom, who got all the brands of food that she enjoyed, loved it.

I also needed to reduce the number I times I had to run to the pharmacy to pick up prescriptions and supplies. I began using the telephone or online refill programs, and the 90-day supply of pills. If you ask physicians to write the prescription for a longer period than the more normal 30 days, usually they will unless there is a compelling reason why it can't be done.

In arranging for a more effective, more stress-free handling of the errands attendant to my Mom's care, I could focus more freely on her well-being *and* mine. Again, self-care is a significant, indeed, essential aspect of caring for others.

In the following, I share my list of self-care, stress-relieving activities;

> 1) *Having a spa day* – Manicures, pedicures, and massages can be emotionally as well as physically restorative. I never used to be a big fan of pampering myself as I felt it was a waste of time and that the money could be better

spent. I also didn't think I deserved treating myself. All that has changed and now, on occasion, I indulge myself, allowing others to pamper me. (One of my doctors has recommended monthly messages as treatment for my neck and spine. I'm all for it. It will help me, keeping me relaxed for interactions with my Mom.) During the spa treatment, make an effort to think of yourself. In other words, be fully present in the moment with and for yourself, taking a mental and emotional inventory, thinking your thoughts, feeling your feelings. You also can recreate the spa treatment at home by lighting candles, playing soft music, and taking a bath of soothing salts or scented oils.

2) *Sitting quietly* – Collect your thoughts, consciously recall wonderful memories, endearing moments with the family, or satisfying past or anticipated vacations. Formerly, as one who worked more than 15 hours a day, nearly 7 days a week, I never knew how to sit quietly. In July of 2012, after a period of earnest reflection, I made some important life decisions, significantly reducing my weekly hours of work. Within the first month, I taught myself to enjoy (and I'll use what I consider an iconic phrase) the sound of silence, turning off my IPhone and laptop, unplugging from the ever-present, ever-intrusive cyber-world of instant, constant communication, taking time for myself, *being* with myself. It's done wonders for me.

3) *Taking a walk* – Walking, the most natural of physical acts, is invigorating and restorative. Walking allows us at a slower, calmer pace to perceive, to "take in" (to exercise our physical senses, seeing, hearing, smelling, touching, even tasting) the fast-paced world that whizzes by (as we race through our day). Walking, in that way, putting us in closer touch with our world around us, can be inspiring and spiritually reviving. Walking, as an act of care for others, also can be self-expansive, granting us opportunities to extend ourselves for the sake of others. In love and respect for (and now in memory of) my sister Renee, I've completed six 50K walking MS marathons, the benefits of which are numerous – raising money for research, treatment, and to find a cure; training and preparing that are boons to personal health; taking time to focus on the people and places, and the nature along the way, thus, freeing my mind, if only for a moment, from my concerns, my worries.

4) *Go Shopping* – Shopping need not be a frivolous, selfish or expensive option, for it need not involve spending money. Shopping, however, does require going out into the marketplace. In that public space, we can see others (people-watching can be a fascinating activity!), see the new styles and colors, and see ourselves in a new way, perhaps trying on some new clothes (which we don't have to buy!). My friends will tell you that I don't like to shop. Over the past couple of years,

however, I've come to enjoy looking around the store, even and especially when I don't plan to buy. I have also discovered that shopping can be an act of freedom from myself in the same way that I, as a kid, dressed up and, for an instant, pretended to be someone else.

5) *Phoning a friend* – As one who loves to talk, this is one of my favorites. At the same time, although I don't always like talking on the phone (for it lacks the immediacy of face-to-face encounter), when I'm sad or overwhelmed, I long to hear the voice of a friend, giving sound advice or helping me to make a decision or saying something humorous to make me laugh.

6) *Go to the movies* – I don't go to the movies that often, yet as a two hour occasion to examine and engage in the lives of others, it can be quite a useful distraction from the worries that constantly attend being a caregiver. The huge screens in movie theaters can be captivating and engrossing. Even a movie on cable TV can provide hours of freedom from the present and all of the challenges that come with it.

7) *Reading a book* – I love the way I feel when I read. Whether the book is non-fiction or business-related, as opposed to the mystery novels I most enjoy, reading compels me to step outside of myself, to stand in another world of my imagination where I meet and

engage new people (the characters in the story), come to know and like (and dislike!) them, and wonder what will happen next. Reading also allows me to attend to other facets of my life aside from thoughts about my Mom and her care.

8) *Watching a comedy* – As a person who tends toward the serious, I don't usually watch comedies. Still, I have discovered that if I am worried, concerned or aggravated about something having to do with my Mom or anyone and anything else, I watch a sit-com, allowing myself a 30 minute period of unrestrained laughter.

9) *Looking at old photos* – This has been a real saving grace for me! Photos evoke my sentimental spirit, allowing me to reminiscence about my family and me through all of my past days and times, good and bad, joyful and sorrowful, and in that act of soulful reflection, reconstituting myself (ironically, perhaps, seeing myself again for the first time) in the present moment. Also, looking at photos with my Mom is a great bonding time for us, for, with her still intact long term memory, she remembers everyone she sees. I'm always amazed when I listen to her announce all the names of the people in the photos, who they were in relation to us, and what was going on in the photo. In that way, she, even suffering from dementia, grants me an open window through which I can view my history and heritage.

10) *Crying when you need to* – As a person with my medical history, involving periods when the question wasn't about whether I would get well, but rather whether I would survive, I have the decidedly "stiff-upper lip." I tend to take life as it comes, tackling the obstacles as they arise and taking advantage of the opportunities when they appear. So, it took me a long time to realize that there is nothing wrong with crying. Crying, I have discovered, can serve as an essential release of pent-up emotions that, if left to fester inside, can grow into larger, corrosive ill feelings. Sometimes, when talking to my closest, dearest friends, as my feelings and frustrations well up and pour out, I find myself crying spontaneously. In that moment, I always feel much better, cleansed of all that ails me.

I designed my Top 10 List after the pattern David Letterman uses on his nightly show. I've done and do other things to take great care of myself, but these are my ten favorite things. I encourage you, if you've not yet made the conscious effort, to discern and decide what your favorite things are that you can do to care for yourself. The most important word of advice I've already shared: *do* use those practices that restore balance to your life and regenerate vitality. We are so busy living our lives and working, not to mention caring for our loved ones, so we may feel that there's little or no time to take care of ourselves too. But we must remember, we can't be of much help to others unless we are in good shape mentally and physically. So take the time and make the effort! You're worth it!

Chapter IX - Dying in Secret

In league with my Mom's fear of not knowing what she's doing, when I contemplate my health, at times, I dread what the future may hold. I'm only 53, but I'm beginning to have concerns about reaching my sixties. My Aunt Diane, shortly after her 60th birthday, received her colon cancer diagnosis that proved to be fatal. In 2010, after my sister's 60th birthday, her MS began to progress more rapidly. I believe that my Mom, now 83, will live a very long time, perhaps another twenty years. In light of my medical history and that of my immediate family, I am committed to doing all that I can to remain healthy. It's something Renee and I frequently discussed and pledged to each other.

When Renee's health hurriedly began to decline, I debated with myself about whether I should take our Mom to California to see her older daughter one last time. (By 2010, my Mom no longer remembered that she was afraid of flying!) I decided against that idea after Nia and I used Skype to connect Renee and Mom. The experience frightened her. Renee's speech was so slurred, making it nearly impossible to understand what she was saying beyond, "Hi, Mom," that Mom believed that she was drunk.

In March of 2011, Nia and I had a small "party" for Renee's 61st birthday, most likely knowing it would be her last birthday celebration. We wore silly birthday hats and brought her exactly what she wanted, a huge carrot cake cupcake! Renee glowed as we sang "Happy Birthday!" I recorded our celebration. On the now countless occasions I've watched the video, I am so very grateful for that day and time. Equally, I am saddened that I did not bring our Mom to share in so joyously poignant a moment.

Sadness, too, fills my heart when I consider that I never showed my Mom the video of Renee's birthday. I wonder why. Throughout, Renee smiled, saying very little, save the joyous word, "Yea!" So I doubt she would be frightened as was her previous reaction to the Skype-experiment. One day, I may show it to my Mom, although I have little idea how she might react.

On July 16, when I arrived in Renee's nursing home room, she smiled weakly and said, "Hi, Loret," which was what she always called me. She tried to say more, so I bent down to listen. "Mom," she said. Assuming that she wanted to know how our Mom was, I said, "She's doing fine." Renee nodded. She then said, "Love." I told her I would tell our Mom that she loved her. She nodded more vigorously. I tried not to cry, but it was hard. With all the turmoil that occurred between my sister and our mother throughout Renee's adolescence, and, later, during her adult years, I was thrilled that she longed to tell our Mom of her love for her. In that moment, another thought occurred. In late 2010, we, in a family conference, had discussed bringing Renee back to Maryland *and* placing her in Mamie's Loving Care with our Mom. In some respects I was sorry that such a reunion never happened. However, I did wonder how our Mom would have reacted to having Renee live in the same place. Given how much Renee had changed in her appearance and in her mobility, I'm not sure our Mom would have known her own daughter. I also don't know how Renee might have reacted to our Mom's current state of mind.

The very next day, on July 17, 2011, my sister and only sibling died of progressive Multiple Sclerosis. It was one of the worst days of my life. I called my relatives, starting with my husband Tim and my Aunt Frannie, who, I knew would call everyone else, for I didn't feel like talking to anyone. For my closest friends, I sent a group text message, believing that they would understand. My greatest concern of the day was whether to tell my Mom. For at least two years, she had not asked about Renee, so I was leaning strongly against telling her. To this day, I've never told her that my sister, *her daughter* died. When I talked to my Mom's friend Mrs. Adams, I shared with her why I didn't want to tell my Mom. She understood. Given my Mom's behavioral pattern of repetition, I thought that telling her about Renee's death might provoke a repetitive cycle of sorrow, a constant, inconsolable grief. I did not want that for my Mom. I consulted Dr. Coerver who agreed that Renee's death was not information that my Mom needed to know. I was relieved. Yet I have felt the discomfort associated with keeping this secret from my Mom.

I'm starting to wonder if my Mom remembers that she had two children. In January 2012, my daughter Kim, my four week old granddaughter Kendal, and my niece Nia visited my Mom. One of the most important reasons for us to be together was to take a four-generation photo. All went well, yet there was heartbreak. My Mom didn't remember Kim or Nia. My Mom had chatted with them, laughing freely. She seemed to enjoy holding Kendal. She appreciated the photos we took. Yet as we prepared to depart, Nia said, "Grandma doesn't remember us." "Of course she remembers you," I replied. Returning to the dining room to rejoin Kim and my Mom, I asked her to name the two women with whom she was speaking. She couldn't. I was stunned!

Kim and Nia seemed to understand that my Mom didn't remember them. I, however, was just devastated. A few months before, I had taken Nia to visit my Mom. When I asked my Mom, "Do you know who this is?" Happily, she replied, "Nia!" She hadn't seen her granddaughter in more than three years, so I was delighted that she remembered her. Now, here it was just a few months later and she couldn't recall. "Nia is Renee's daughter," I added, hoping to jog whatever semblance or remainder of memory my Mom possessed. Her only response? "Oh!" She didn't ask, as I expected (as I had prayed), "Who's Renee?" That scared me and broke my heart, for my Mom might forget me, too. Is it possible for her to forget one child but not the other? It's a selfish thought. I *never* want to think that I am forgettable. Yet, when it comes to dementia, everyone can be and *will* be beyond the grasp of memory.

Chapter X - Mom's Best Quotes

When my Mom's doctor first said the word "dementia" to us, I remember dropping my head instantly overcome with anxiety about the future. My Mom looked at me and asked, "That's bad isn't it?" With the most positive tone I could muster attempting to mask my fear, I said, "Yes, but there are worse things." With no hesitation, my Mom quickly asked, "Besides dying, what's worse than not being able to remember anything?" Even though I've always believed that I have an answer for everything, I had no answer to that question.

Because her question was so profound, and so profoundly affected me, from that moment on, I began writing down the things my Mom asked or said. The following quotes are some of her best words through which she, through the shadow of her dementia, shines a light of surest wisdom and truest humor.

****

In 2006, during a routine doctor's visit, my Mom stopped breathing, and her pulse barely registered. A Code Blue was called and through the swift and skilled attention of the doctor and staff, she was revived. Later, when I explained to her what happened, she, remembering nothing of it, with a look of purest wonderment exclaimed, "Wow, that's amazing, I slept right through dying!"

****

After my Mom lost her way in Providence Hospital I
vowed that I would never let her out of my sight,
especially in a large building or vast area. When I couldn't
go with my Mom to her next appointment, Tim happily
volunteered to accompany her. I demanded of him that
he "keep his eyes on her at all times." He promised that
he would. At the end of my Mom's appointment, she had
to use the restroom before the ride home. When she came
out, noticing Tim's position standing close to the
restroom door and his posture of vigilance, she said to
him, "I guess Loretta told you I got lost, huh?" Tim
nodded, and then told her that I had threatened to kill
him if he came home without her. They laughed
hysterically, and then went to lunch to celebrate her not
getting lost.

****

My Mom and I were discussing our now customary, but
no less aggravating long wait before being seen by her
primary care doctor. My Mom said, "I wish I could forget
how long we've been waiting. How come the dementia
doesn't kick in when I want it to?" I truly had no answer
for that, but we giggled for a long time while we waited.

****

Providence Hospital has a lovely gift shop with a wide
array of merchandise, all of it attractively displayed. On
every trip to the hospital, we visited the gift shop so that
my Mom could select her favorite candy. Each time, it
was the same scenario: she'd declare that she had no
money with her, and I would tell her not to worry and

that she still could still get her favorite candy bar. On one visit, she said, "Oh then I'll get a few more things since you're paying. I'll start leaving my purse at home more often too!" She then proceeded to fill up a basket with candy of every kind and size, not realizing that she hadn't carried her purse for years.

****

In January of 2008, as part of my birthday celebration, Tim, Kim, my Mom, and I went to an upscale restaurant in downtown D.C. My Mom eats very slowly, unless it's dessert, which when it was served, she quickly consumed. Almost immediately she asked, "Can we get dessert?" I answered, "You just had dessert." Narrowing her eyes, she looked at me with distrust and said, "I did? What did I have?" I showed her the photo of her enjoying her dessert. She said, "Oh that looks good! Did I like it?" Assuring her that she loved it, she quickly replied, "I'd love to have a bite of that picture, too!"

****

My mom loves sweets more than anything else. The bakery, Cake Love, is a few miles from her group home. Whenever we go there, she grumbles loudly about the $5 price of a cupcake. Once she takes her first bite, she literally swallows all of her complaints proclaiming, "This is the best cupcake *ever*! Why haven't you brought me here before?" The clerks, who know my Mom well, for we go to the bakery often, smile and say, "See ya' next time, Ms. Doris!" She yells back, "OK, see ya' next time!" I'd buy her a million cupcakes if only she could remember the next time.

****

After my Mom first began to forget things, I was excited that she remembered to go down the hall from her apartment to attend her favorite Tuesday and Thursday Tai Chi class. When I commented that she had gone to the class without being reminded she said, "Oh don't worry, I only forget the things I don't like anyway. I'd never forget Tai Chi."

And up until the last few months she lived in the retirement community, she never forgot to go to the class.

****

As we were returning home from a doctor's appointment, my Mom asked, "When is our next appointment?" I told her she was doing so well that it wouldn't be for another six months. She replied, "That's still too soon. I need to get healthier so I can cut my schedule back. There are way *too* many things on my calendar." My only thought; was "Really? What things?"

****

We were stopped at a red light and a woman walking three dogs on leashes crossed the street in front of our car. My Mom said, "I didn't used to like dogs did I?" I confirmed that she had always been afraid of dogs since she was a little girl. "OK," she responded, "I was just checking. I still don't like dogs." "OK," I said, "you don't have to like dogs." She look puzzled for a minute and then asked, "I don't have a dog do I?" Assuring her that she didn't, she seemed relieved and said, "Good, 'cause I'd have to go home and give it away since I don't like dogs."

****

In February of 2009, for her birthday, I gave my Mom a pair of house shoes, which just happened to be called Memory Foam slippers. My Mom apparently assuming that I had bought them to help her memory in some way, asked, "How is something I wear on my feet gonna help what's wrong with my brain?" Again, I had no answer for that.

****

We were in line at a McDonald's, my Mom's favorite restaurant since being diagnosed with dementia. I ordered sensible salads for us. She asked if she could have an apple pie, I said. "Of course, you have to eat all of your lunch first." The cashier chuckled at my comment, prompting my Mom to say "We've switched roles, I used to be her Mom, and now she's mine."

****

On the day I moved my Mom to the group home, I was asked to leave quickly so she could get acclimated to her new surroundings. I was worried about leaving her, but wanted to follow the rules as they were presented to me. As I was about to leave, preparing for a long good-bye, I said to my Mom, "I'm going to leave so you can get settled in your new place, OK?" My Mom was sitting and eating cookies with Ms. Mamie, the proprietor, and Angelina, the primary caregiver. Barely looking up at me and said, "Ok, bye." I was a little hurt by her quick dismissal, so I said, "Do I get a goodbye hug?" and she said, "I'll hug you next time, I'm eating cookies right now." I never thought a cookie would stand in the way of me getting a hug!

****

A routine trip to the grocery store, during the time that I still allowed my Mom to write checks, turned into one of those "aha moments". When we got in line to pay for our items, she asked me, "What's today?" I answered her. Unfortunately, the line was very long, so my Mom asked me repeatedly. Each time I answered. When we finally got to the counter, she asked a final time, "What's today?" Before I could answer, several people in the long line replied loudly and in unison, "It's the 17th!" My Mom looked surprised, and then said, "I guess I've asked what day it is already, huh?" I confirmed that she had. As she giggled at that thought, she mumbled, "Sorry."

As we were leaving the store, a woman asked if she could give me a hug and wanted to know how I keep my patience with my Mom, not once becoming angry with her, yelling at her, or telling her to be quiet. The woman was in tears and told me that she had learned so much from me observing the two of us, and that she was going to try to be more patient and loving with her own mother. It gladdened my heart to know that Mom and I could be an inspiration to someone else's family also struggling with this disease.

****

While shopping, my Mom was overwhelmed by the very reasonable Walmart prices (1970 prices are what she remembers). She assumed that I was rich simply because I was willing to pay $19 for a pair of pajamas. When she overheard another woman also complaining about the costs, my Mom said to her, "My daughter is rich. She buys me everything. She can pay for your stuff, too." The lady said to my Mom, "You're lucky. Your daughter must really love you." My Mom replied, "Yep, and it's good to have people love you because they buy you lots of stuff." The lady looked at me, smiled and said, "You're doing a wonderful job with your mother."

****

In 2010, Tim turned 60. Our daughter Kim made an incredible cake for him, a golf lover if there ever was one, shaped like a golf course, complete with a water hazard, flags, a sand trap, and even "rocks" made of chocolate. As my Mom is such a dessert person, she was excited about getting a piece of this incredible cake. When Kim sliced the cake, she made certain that my Mom got all of the elements. When she saw the "rocks" on the cake, she asked "What are these?" I replied, "They're chocolate rocks and you can eat them." Trusting me implicitly, she grabbed one of the rocks and popped it into her mouth. She smiled broadly and said, "This is the best rock I ever had! If I had known rocks were that good, I would have let you eat them when you were little." I didn't feel it necessary to tell her that those were different kinds of rocks and it was a good thing that I hadn't eaten them.

****

In the spring of 2011, I picked up my Mom and drove two miles to a beautiful harbor nearby so we could walk along the water. She asked, "Where we were going?" "For a walk," I said. She thought for a moment and said, "If we are going for a walk, then why are we in the car?" I laughed so hard I had to pull over so I wouldn't have an accident.

****

In December 2011, Kim (who my Mom no longer remembers without reminders, and when prompted only remembers her as a teenager) had a little girl named Kendal. I showed my Mom a picture of Kim with our new grandbaby. My Mom said, "Where did she get that baby?" "She had the baby," I replied. "She's a little young to have a baby isn't she?" "Mom, Kim's 40 years old". "Oh," she replied, "I guess I missed a few years." "A *few*?" I thought to myself, "It's closer to twenty-five."

****

After church on Christmas Day, we took my Mom to see the new Martin Luther King Jr. Monument along the Potomac River on the National Mall. We walked through the entire grounds of the memorial, reading all of the quotes, which my Mom recited aloud. She seemed very proud. As we looked around, she said, "I never thought I'd live to see a MLK monument." "Nor I," I replied. As I took her picture next to MLK's statue, I asked her if she believed the statue looked like MLK and she responded, "It looks just like him, but I don't remember him being that tall!" I laugh hysterically every time I think of that day.

****

My mom is virtually a little kid now. I have to watch everything she does. She loves the old-fashioned penny candy. Whenever I go to Cracker Barrel, I get her a bag of one of her favorites, Mary Jane or Bit of Honey. I've had to learn to give her only one or two pieces, and then put the rest away. If she has the big bag, she will open it, take one out, eat it, close it and say, "I'll save the rest for later". But that event plays itself out over and over until the bag is nearly empty. When I remind her of how many she's eaten, she says, "I didn't eat all those by myself. Didn't I share some with you?" Needless to say, I have to inform her that she did *not* share any of her candy with me!

****

I went to my Mom's group home on a Wednesday, dropping off some prescriptions and advising the caregiver and my Mom that I was going to pick her up on Friday to take her out for lunch. My Mom looked puzzled. Thinking that she was trying to figure out when Friday was, I said, "Friday is two days from now." "I know," she said, "I'm just trying to figure out if that's enough time for me to get ready". Is my Mom turning into a diva now?

****

For most of my life, my Mom's favorite candy has been a Kit Kat bar. I have traveled to many places in the world, and I've always brought her samples of the candy from other countries. Although, she's been intrigued by the package written in other languages, she still recognizes it as her favorite Kit Kat bar. We recently went "shopping" at CVS and I told her she could pick out her favorite candy. For a long while, she scanned the row upon row of candies, seemingly waiting for her favorite to jump up and reveal itself to her. But to my real surprise, she didn't remember it. I pointed to the Kit Kat and said, "That's your favorite". "OK, thanks," she said and picked up the candy. As we moved toward the checkout line, she said, "Wait, we better get two of them because, if it is my favorite, one isn't enough". "Fair enough," I said, "You can have two".

****

My Mom still has a full head of hair. To manage her, at times, unruly mane, I told her caregiver to pull her hair back into a ponytail. I was thought that my Mom wouldn't mind or wouldn't remember that she wasn't a ponytail kind of girl. However, she *did* remember, pulling off the bands that held her hair in place. In light of her "ponytail rejection", occasionally I take her to get her hair done. It's amazing to me that she remembers how she likes her hair and flat out refuses to have it done any other way. As soon as the hairdresser is done, my Mom looks in the mirror and then styles her hair the way she likes it. Our hairdresser just stands back and smiles. Before we leave, my Mom always says, "Next time, *don't* forget how I like my hair, I *don't* like it in my face". Attuned to the irony, I think to myself, "Mom, should you *really* accuse someone of not remembering things?"

****

Trying to dress an 83 year old who still has a mind of her own can be tough. That's what my Mom's caregivers face on a daily basis. On most days, they lay out her clothes. However, because she can still dress herself, she usually will insist on wearing what she desires. Preparing for our lunch date, her caregiver and I searched my Mom's closet trying to find something appropriate for her to wear. Suddenly, my Mom said, "Shouldn't I be the one looking for an outfit since I'm the one who'll be wearing it?" We turned to look at her and burst into laughter. Simply put, she wore what she wanted to wear.

****

My Mom always has loved to read. Whenever you see her, usually she has a magazine or a book in her hands. Once the dementia became more pronounced, she still remembered her passion for reading, *but*, in spite of her many volumes, she now tends to read the same book over and over. Recently, her favorite book is "How To Keep The Brain Active". I asked her if it was good. She replied, "It's not just a great book, it also keeps me from forgetting stuff". I thought to myself, "Given that you've already read that book more than fifteen times, maybe we should ask for our money back."

****

Occasionally, I wonder about how my Mom will die. I suppose that many people ponder the deaths – the when, the how – of their loved ones. As the women in our family tend to live a long time (my great grandmother lived to be 106), I believe that my Mom, even at age 83, still has many years before her life ends.

That said, my Mom loves food so much that I suppose she could eat herself to death if no one watched her. Her favorite conversation with her primary caregiver is about food. Typically, she eats three meals a day. Usually, within half hour, she will ask, "Is it time to eat?" Her caregiver will remind her that she has just eaten. Then, my Mom will ask, "What did I eat?" Her caregiver will describe the meal in detail. Still my Mom not only doesn't remember eating any meals, she seemingly no longer has the feeling of being full. She will always say, "Are you sure that was today? It feels like I haven't eaten since yesterday".

Although I, at times, contemplate my Mom's death and often worry about her forgetfulness in relation to her craving of food, still I look forward to hearing her say, "Is it time to eat yet?"

****

After eating at least six cookies before I took the package away my Mom asked, "Can I just have one more cookie? Please? After all, I haven't had that many and life is short." Good one Mom!

****

I asked my Mom to tell me in one word the name of her favorite food. We play these kinds of games all the time to keep her mind active. I didn't think this was a hard question at all, but she seemed to struggle with it. Suddenly, she smiled, happily blurting out, "All! That's one word. Right?" I rolled on the floor laughing. "Well," she explained, "that was a hard question because I couldn't just think of one kind of food. I like it *all!*" I told her she did a fabulous job with the question.

****

I picked up my Mom for a doctor's appointment. As we get in the car, she asks, "Can we skip the doctor's appointment and go to lunch instead?"

****

We were at the very reasonably-priced Olive Garden for lunch. My Mom says, "With these prices, this food better be the best I've ever had!" I've given up trying to teach my

Mom the current price structures and just go with the flow. Thankfully, she loved her lunch.

****

I took my Mom out to lunch and our waiter asked, "Can I tell you about the specials for today?" Before she could continue my Mom asked, "Are the specials about dessert?" "No," the waiter answered, "but I'll certainly tell you about dessert after you're done with the entrees." My Mom then said emphatically, "Then I don't want to hear about the specials. Just give me chicken!" I shook my head in disbelief, and the waitress burst out laughing, saying, "I totally understand."

After my Mom finished her chicken, the waiter offered a fabulous presentation of the "dessert specials," which included a little dance. My Mom was thrilled and clapped enthusiastically. It got even better when my Mom said, "It all looks so good I can't decide. Can I have a little piece of everything?" "Of course, you can," the waiter replied, beaming. Soon, she returned with an amazing plate of individual squares of every dessert. My Mom was in heaven *and* I gave the waiter the largest tip I've *ever* given.

****

I always tell my Mom that she has to finish her meal before she can have dessert. One day while we were out to lunch, she said that she was full, but still had half a sandwich to finish. While I was sending a text message, out of the corner of my eye, I saw my Mom wrapping her remaining sandwich in a napkin and about to put it in our bag of trash. "Are you throwing away your sandwich?" I asked. Knowing that she had been "caught", she smiled sheepishly, and then responded, "Ummm, no, I was just saving it to take home so I can get to dessert faster!" I had to laugh thinking about how many times I threw away food on my plate as a kid so I could get to the dessert. I guess even with dementia, you can still remember how to lie.

****

My Mom loves musicals. We watched The King and I, one of her all-time favorites. We both loved Yul Brynner, so I was excited to watch it again. At some point, my Mom said, "This is such a great movie. I can't believe I've never seen it before." She asked, "What year was this movie made?" I answered that I didn't know the exact year, but I believed it was made in the 1950s. She replied, "Oh, good! I'm glad it was just a few years ago. Maybe he will make more movies. I love his bald head." I didn't have the heart to tell her that the only movies Yul Brynner would make would be in heaven.

****

As I was packing to move my Mom to her new home, her bookcase filled with her books needed to be downsized. I told her she could pick ten books to take with her, and that I'd keep the remaining volumes safe at my house. She said, "Only ten books? How am I going to survive on that?" I told her that we could exchange some of the books whenever she wanted, so she would always have variety of choice. She thought for a minute and said, "Good, because I'd die if I had to read the same ten books over and over!" I started to laugh, almost falling to the floor. Why? Because my Mom reads all the time, but in the three years she's been in her group home, she's had the ten books she selected, but has only read the same two books over and over. When I suggest that she begin reading one of the other eight books, she says, "No, I don't want to confuse myself until I finish what I'm reading now." I always reply, "OK".

****

My Mom and I had visited my friend Pat in Georgetown Hospital. Because of the heavy traffic, I turned off the main road, driving on an unfamiliar street. Suddenly, my Mom yelled, "Stop!" I did. My Mom pointed at a row house and said, "Grandma used to live here". "What?" I said. I never had heard this story. I called my Aunt Frannie, our family historian, and gave her the address of the house. Frannie confirmed that my great grandmother *did* live in that house when she and my Mom were teenagers. Frannie and I were shocked that my Mom remembered that. In an exasperated tone my Mom asked, "Why did you have to check what I said? Didn't you believe me? I have a great memory!" I apologized for doubting her. Truly, I was impressed that she remembered the address of a place that was a part of our family history dating back to the 1930s. I was also distressed that she no longer remembered the address of the home in which I was born in 1959 or the home she lives in now.

****

During our 25th wedding anniversary reception, Tim and I wanted to ensure that everyone got up and danced and had a good time, including my Mom who at that time was 81 years old. She began to dance with me and looked to be having a ball. After a while, I began to worry that she would get tired. I said to her, "You've danced for a long time. Do you want to take a break for a few minutes?" "No," she said, "I'm fine. I only remember dancing one song anyway, so I forget to be tired."

****

Thinking it would be good for my Mom to get out for a couple of days a week to be with other seniors, I enrolled her in an adult day care program. It was fairly expensive, but I figured my Mom was more than worth it. The problem was that she hated it. She wanted to sit by herself and read a book, while the day care folks wanted her to be involved in activities throughout the day. Understanding and accepting how she felt, I took her out of the program. When I told her she that didn't have to return, she said, "Thank goodness, I don't know *what* you were thinking. I'm way too old for day care."

****

My Mom was having a really tough day and was confused about everything that happened. Seeking to end our time together on a positive note, I got us both ice cream cones, which we thoroughly enjoyed. As I parked in front of the group home, my Mom asked, "Is this where I live?" This was my Mom's second year of residency, so I was a little surprised by her question. "Yes", I answered, "this is where you live." As we got out of the car my Mom said, "Thanks for the ice cream." "You remember the ice cream?" I asked. "I just don't remember where I live," she replied, "but, *of course*, I remember the ice cream." We laughed hysterically.

****

After my Mom had been at the group home nearly two years, the owner, Ms. Mamie, called me to say that due to renovations, they were moving her to the bedroom across the hall. Mom's neurologist had suggested that once a person with dementia gets settled, changes should be made only if absolutely necessary. Although I gave Ms. Mamie permission to move my Mom, I wasn't sure how well it would work out. It didn't work out. Not at all. At some point during each night, my Mom would cross the hallway, returning to her old room, and, in the process, disturbing everyone. Finally, when my Mom was informed that the experiment of "moving her" to a new bedroom was over and that she'd stay in her original room, she said, "Good! Don't try to move me anymore". How ironic. On most days, when you ask my Mom which room is hers, she can't tell you.

****

After I completed the 2010 MS 50K two-day Marathon, Tim brought my Mom to the closing ceremonies that were held on the lawn of the U.S. Capitol. As I received my medal my family and friends cheered. My Mom applauded, too yelling, "Yea, Retta!" However, she hadn't understood what I had done. She asked Tim why everyone was cheering. Tim told her I had just finished a marathon. "Oh," she said, "that's big! I've gotta cheer louder!" So, she increased the volume of her, "Yea Retta!"

****

The Conclusion as of the end of 2012

When I was a kid, I never thought about taking care of my Mom. I don't think any child, even when reaching the adult years, thinks about it. Even as I watched my Mom take care of my grandparents, especially my grandmother, it never crossed my mind. I always thought I had plenty of time to worry about that. The women in our family lived long lives, so I was counting on my Mom remaining self-sufficient even into her 90's. This had been the pattern for my great grandmother and my grandmother. Both were fairly healthy into their very senior years. My great grandmother, Luray White, died in a nursing home at the age of 106, and my grandmother died at home of colon cancer at age 90.

On the rare occasions that I did think about my Mom aging, I still believed that she would continue to live on her own for years in her retirement community, enjoying her Tai Chi classes. But that was not to be. My Mom is the first female in our family to suffer from dementia, so there was no roadmap or anyone within the family from whom to seek guidance.

Just when I was starting to think about what the next steps would be for my Mom if she needed care outside of her retirement community, I had my own health crisis. From 1988 until 2001, I was concerned about my own survival. Any thoughts I had about caring for my Mom in the future were pushed aside. My only consideration about my Mom was how she would cope if I died. On repeated reflection, it had become clear to me that my love and concern for her were the primary motivations for my determination to live.

I envy the people who don't have to experience the heartbreak of caring for their parents. Tim's mother died a couple of years before we got married. His father, who had taken care of all of his final arrangements died in 1991. All that was required of us was to call an 800 number. Had Tim needed to assist in taking care of his parents, he would have shared the weight and wealth of that responsibility with his siblings.

The most unsettling thing for me is the reality that aside from my very willing husband, I'm pretty much alone in caring for my Mom. I'm already planning what may be next for her should she require a greater level of care than the group home can provide. As a first step, I'm taking on a new job in addition to my consulting business to save more funds for my Mom's future needs. I suppose I knew early on that her retirement check was not going to be enough to finance her long term care, but I didn't act quickly enough. I wish all housing options for our elderly had a reduced rent program like my Mom's former retirement community, but they don't. Dementia type care is very expensive, and although I'm saving as much money as I can in IRAs and 401Ks for Tim and me to be prepared for our retirement that does absolutely nothing for my Mom.

Each time I see my Mom, I think to myself, "Why isn't my Aunt Diane or my sister Renee here with me?" The three of us should be laughing together at my Mom's hysterical sayings or crying together when my Mom's frustration about her inability to remember what's she's doing from one minute to the next causes her to yell, "I don't know what I'm doing!" Diane and Renee should still be alive and not only because they promised that we all would take care of my Mom, but also because they were *too* young to die. I'm so afraid of caring for my Mom alone. I worry about making mistakes, perhaps encountering a circumstance where I need more information than I have at my disposal (or, as conceivably, when I *don't know* that I need more information!) and, thus, make a poor or an ineffectual choice. I fret about saying or doing, or not saying or doing something that upsets my Mom. Every day, I wrestle with these fears.

Watching my Mom and her many childlike behaviors is like watching my amazing granddaughter Kendal, but in reverse. At eleven months old, Kendal is crawling around at a fast pace, but is standing unassisted and very close to walking. She likes to scoot around in her walker, her little legs churning, anxious to go as fast as possible. At eighty-three, my Mom, always swift on her feet, can out-walk almost anyone her age. She suffers from no arthritis. She doesn't have a limp or a cane. Yet, as an elderly person, I realize that she's one fall away from breaking her hip, and eventually needing assistance to move about. When Kendal comes to visit, eagerly I attend to her needs, even the diaper changes for I know it is a part of life *and* that it only needs to be done for a limited period of time. I pray that if or when that time comes for my Mom, I will be able to change her diapers with the same attentive care that I have for my granddaughter.

When I look back at my Mom's life, several things come to mind. Her anxieties prevented her from achieving her junior high school dreams of traveling the world, journeying to see all the places she learned about in geography and yearned to see and experience for herself. Her only marriage failed through no fault of her own. Raising two kids as a single mother, and being at her government employee grade level didn't allow for her to save additional money for her retirement. Still, there are quite a few plusses regarding her current condition. Most notably, my Mom enjoys wide coverage under her medical insurance policy, which is a tremendous help. Another amazing blessing is that my Mom is oblivious to almost all of the unusual or horrible things that happen daily. The August 2011 earthquake that rattled the entire mid-Atlantic coastline, the August 2012 tragic shootings at the Aurora, Colorado, movie theater, and the incredible damage done to the Northeast region by Super Storm Sandy didn't affect her at all, whereas my pre-dementia Mom would have been upset for days afterwards. There really can be blessings in all things.

I believe the only thing my Mom ever wanted out of life was to be loved and respected and to live with dignity and with all her written instructions followed. For the rest of her life I will ensure that she gets exactly what she wants, because she gave birth to me and I love her with all my heart. While I was never blessed with giving birth to children of my own, God has entrusted me with being my Mom's mom. No matter what awaits me and my Mom in the future, I pray that I'll continue to have the love, strength, and courage to be the best mom for her I can be.

Family Photos

Sneaking cake on my 1st birthday

Loving ice cream at age 2

First hospitalization at age 4

My 6th birthday celebration

Easy Bake Oven Fun

Family vacation to NY in 1969

My 18th Birthday

My 1980 College Graduation

Our 1985 wedding
Renee, Grandparents Charles and Alberta,
Me, Tim, Mom, Aunt Diane and Nia

Family Photos

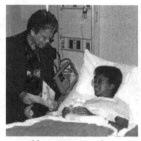

Mom visiting me after
surgery in 1992

Mom, Renee, Nia, Aunt Diane, Me, and
Grandma Alberta on Xmas 1997

Visiting Renee at the
nursing home in 2010

Mom at Tai Chi Class in 2008

Dancing with Mom at our
25th wedding anniversary
celebration in 2010

Mom congratulating me
at the finish line of the
2010 MS Marathon

Mrs. Adams helping Mom
celebrate her 81st birthday

Four generations
Kim, Kendal, Mom and Me

Mom doing her
favorite pastime

References

Alzheimer's Association – www.alz.org

A Place for Mom – www.aplaceformom.com

Dementia Therapy and Music – downloaded from A Place for Mom at http://alzheimers.aplaceformom.com/articles/dementia-therapy-and-music

"How to be more Patient" from Code of Living Self-improvement and Motivation http://www.codeofliving.com/how-be-more-patient

How Animal Therapy Helps Dementia Patients - By Madeline Vann, MPH Medically reviewed by Pat F. Bass III, MD, MPH

http://www.everydayhealth.com/alzheimers/how-animal-therapy-helps-dementia-patients.aspx

Humor Therapy Helps Manage Dementia by Rick Nauert, PhD, Senior News Editor

http://psychcentral.com/news/2011/09/22/humor-therapy-helps-manage-dementia/29692.html

Humor Helps with Dementia Homecaring Duties by Courtney Mroch

http://health.families.com/blog/humor-helps-with-dementia-homecaring-duties

Merriam-Webster Dictionary. www.merriam-websteronline.com